HMH

Assessment Readiness and Practice Tests

Grade 2

Includes:

- Benchmark Tests
- Performance Assessment Tasks
- Test Taking Strategies
- Targeted Practice of Concepts and Skills

Printed in the U.S.A.

ISBN 978-1-328-51915-3

1 2 3 4 5 6 7 8 9 10 0982 27 26 25 24 23 22 21 20 19 18

4500721891 B C D E F G

Contents

Assessment Formats

Many of today's mathematics assessments contain item types beyond the traditional multiple-choice format, which allows for a more robust assessment of children's understanding of concepts.

Many of these mathematics assessments will be administered via computers; and *Assessment Readiness and Practice Tests* presents items in formats similar to what you will see on the tests. The following information is provided to help familiarize you with these different types of items. Each item type is identified on pages (vii–viii). The examples will introduce you to the item types.

The following explanations are provided to guide you in answering the questions. These pages (v–vi) describe the most common item types. You may find other types on some tests.

Example 1 Choose numbers less than a given number.

More Than One Correct Choice

This type of item looks like a traditional multiple-choice item, but it asks you to choose all of something. When the item asks you to find all, look for more than one correct choice. Carefully look at each choice and mark it if it is a correct answer.

Example 2 Choose tens and ones to describe a number.

Choose From a List

Sometimes when you take a test on a computer, you will have to select a word, number, or symbol from a drop-down list. The *Assessment Readiness and Practice Tests* practice tests and worksheets show a list and ask you to choose the correct answer. Make your choice by circling the correct answer. There will only be one choice that is correct.

Example 3 Sort numbers into groups for greater than or less than a given number.

Sorting

You may be asked to sort something into categories. These items will present numbers, words, or equations on rectangular "tiles." The directions will ask you to write each of the items in the box that tells about it.

Sometimes you may write the same number or word in more than one box. For example, if you need to sort quadrilaterals by category, a square could be in a box labeled rectangle and another box labeled rhombus.

Example 4 Order numbers from least to greatest.

Use Given Numbers in the Answer

You may also see numbers and symbols on tiles when you are asked to write an equation or answer a question using only numbers. You should use the given numbers to write the answer to the problem. Sometimes there will be extra numbers. You may also need to use each number more than once.

Example 5 Match related facts.

Matching

Some items will ask you to match equivalent values or other related items. The directions will specify what you should match. There will be dots to guide you in drawing lines. The matching may be between columns or rows.

Item Types:

Example 1

More Than One Correct Choice

Fill in the bubble next to all the correct answers.

Choose all the numbers less than 25.

- ○ 32
- ○ 24
- ○ 52
- ○ 17
- ○ 61

Example 2

Choose From a List

Circle the words.

What is another way to write 24?

2	tens ones	4	tens ones

Example 3

Sorting

Copy the numbers in the right box.

Write each number in the box that tells about it.

33 46 72 97

Less than 50	Greater than 50

Example 4

Use the Numbers

Write the numbers.

Write the numbers in order from least to greatest.

18 12 21 8

____ ____ ____ ____

Example 5

Matching

Draw lines to match.

Match the related facts.

$3 + 2 = 5$ •	• $9 - 6 = 3$
$8 - 2 = 6$ •	• $2 + 3 = 5$
$3 + 6 = 9$ •	• $2 + 7 = 9$
$9 - 7 = 2$ •	• $8 - 6 = 2$

Name ______________________________

Practice Test

Learning Objective
Add and subtract within 100 to solve one- and two-step word problems involving various situations.

1. Jerry picked 16 red apples. He picked 27 green apples. How many apples did Jerry pick?

Label the bar model. Write a number sentence with a ■ for the missing number. Solve.

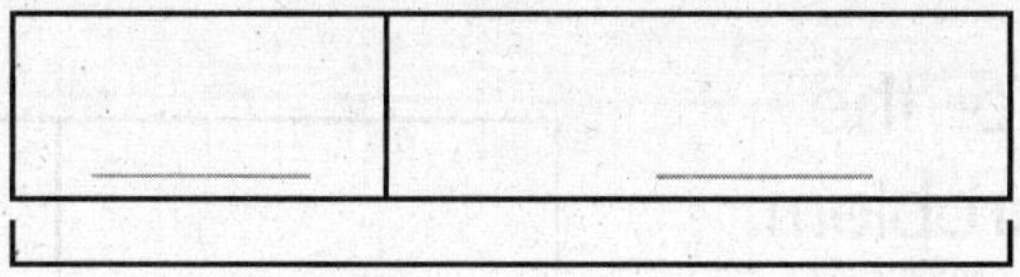

______

______________________________ ______ apples

---

2. George collected 36 oak leaves. He collected 41 maples leaves. Show how you can break apart the addends to show how many leaves George collected.

36 ⟶ ______ + ______

+ 41 ⟶ ______ + ______

______ + ______ = ______

---

3. Ben has 37 pennies. Rachel has 22 pennies. How many pennies do they have?

______ pennies

GO ON

Name ______________________________

4. Kent's book has 64 pages. Kent reads 27 pages in the morning. He reads 18 more pages that night. How many pages does Kent need to read to finish the book?

Complete the bar models for the steps you do to solve the problem.

____	____

______

____	____

______

______ more pages

5. A boat can hold 45 people. 27 more people can fit on the boat. How many people are on the boat now?

Write a number sentence for the problem. Use a ■ for the missing number. Then solve.

____

There are ______ people on the boat.

6. John has 16 rocks. He gives 7 rocks to his cousin. How many rocks does John have now? Write a number sentence for the problem. Use ■ for the missing number. Then solve.

____

______ rocks

STOP

Name ______________________________

Practice Test

Learning Objective
Add and subtract fluently within 20 using mental strategies.

1. Fill in the bubble next to all the doubles facts you could use to find the sum of 4 + 5.

○ 2 + 2

○ 3 + 3

○ 4 + 4

○ 5 + 5

---

2. Which number sentence has the same difference as 15 − 8 = ■?

○ 10 − 1 = ■

○ 10 − 2 = ■

○ 10 − 3 = ■

○ 10 − 4 = ■

---

3. There are 8 large plates and 7 small plates on a table. How many plates are on the table? Write the number sentence. Show how you can make a ten to find the sum. Write the sum.

8 + 7 = ______

10 + ______ = ______

GO ON

Name ______________________________

4. Ling sees 13 birds in a tree and 5 birds on the ground. How many more birds does Ling see in the tree than on the ground? Draw a picture and write a number sentence to solve.

____

_____ more birds

---

5. There are 9 oranges in a bag. Mr. Johnson puts 4 more oranges in the bag. Complete the addition sentence to find how many oranges are in the bag now.

_____ + _____ = _____

_____ oranges

---

6. Use the numbers on the tiles to write the differences. Then write the next fact in the pattern.

6 7 8 9

11 − 3 = _____	10 − 3 = _____
11 − 4 = _____	11 − 3 = _____
11 − 5 = _____	12 − 3 = _____
______________	______________

STOP

Name ____________________

Learning Objective
Determine whether a group of objects, up to 20, has an even or an odd number of members.

1. Choose the ten frame that shows an even number.

○ 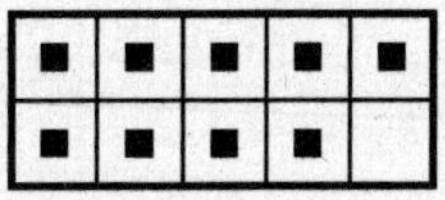

○ 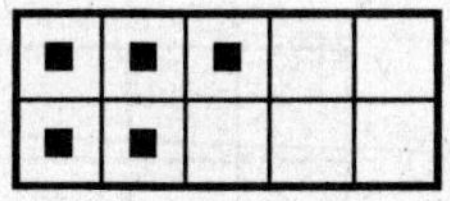

○ 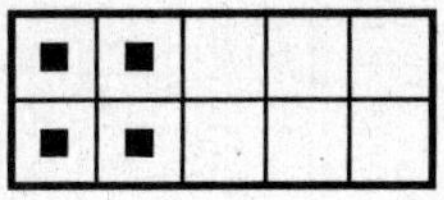

○ 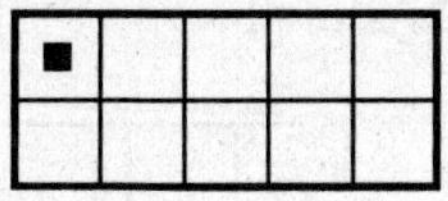

2. Write an even number between 3 and 12.
Draw a picture and then write a sentence to explain why it is an even number.

____

____

3. Mary has an even number of shells and an odd number of rocks. Choose all the groups of shells and rocks that could belong to Mary.

○ 4 shells and 8 rocks

○ 9 shells and 6 rocks

○ 8 shells and 3 rocks

○ 4 shells and 7 rocks

GO ON

Name ____________________

4. Choose the ten frame that shows an odd number.

○ 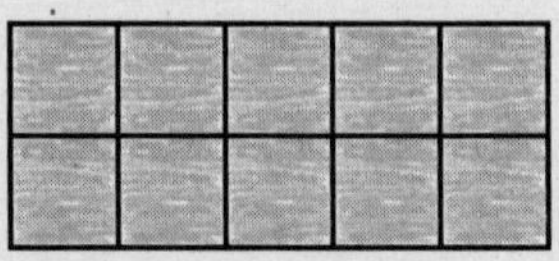

○ 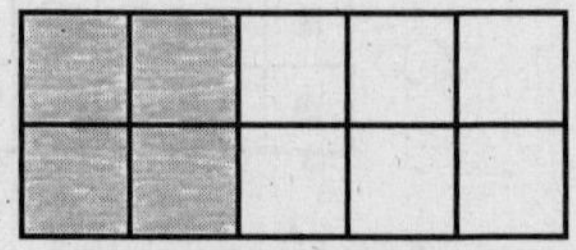

○ 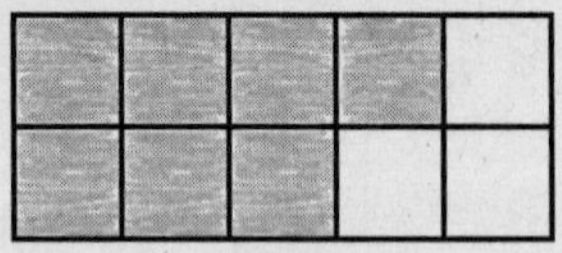

○ 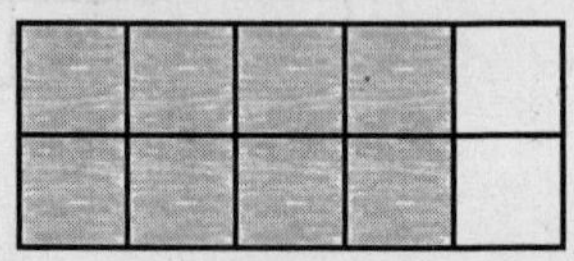

5. Write an even number between 7 and 16. Draw a picture and then write a sentence to explain why it is an odd number.

____

____

6. Ted has an even number of yellow markers and an odd number of green markers. Choose all the groups of markers that could belong to Ted.

○ 8 yellow markers and 3 green markers

○ 3 yellow markers and 6 green markers

○ 4 yellow markers and 2 green markers

○ 6 yellow markers and 7 green markers

STOP

Learning Objective
Add to find the total number of objects in a rectangular array (up to 5 × 5), and write an equation to express the total as a sum of equal addends.

Name ______________________________

1. Find the number of shapes in each row.

3 rows of ______

Complete the addition sentence to find the total.

______ + ______ + ______ = ______

---

2. Max and his sister each have 4 playing cards.
Draw a picture to show the groups of cards.

How many playing cards do they have?

______ playing cards

---

3. Find the number of shapes in each row.

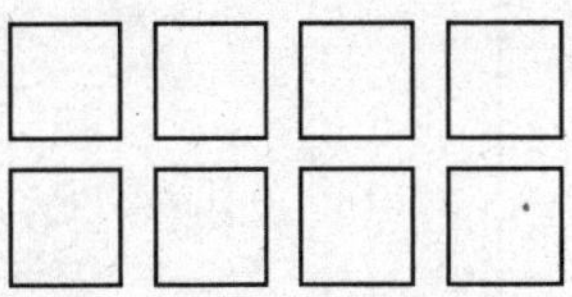

2 rows of ______

Complete the addition sentence to find the total.

______ + ______ = ______

GO ON

Name ______________________________

4. Write how many in each row and in each column.

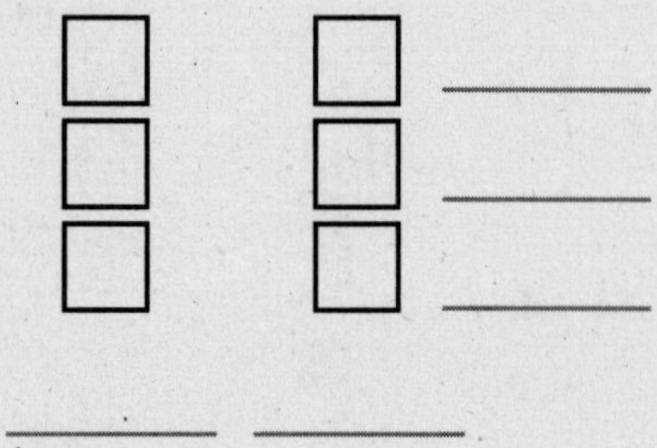

5. Fill in the bubble next to all of the equations that match the array above.

○ $2 + 2 = 4$

○ $3 + 3 = 6$

○ $2 + 2 + 2 = 6$

○ $3 + 3 + 3 = 9$

6. Tanya and 2 friends put rocks on the table. Each person put 2 rocks on the table. Draw a picture to show the groups of rocks.

How many rocks did they put on the table?

_____ rocks

STOP

Name ____________________

Practice Test

Learning Objective
Show that the digits of a three-digit number represent amounts of hundreds, tens, and ones.

1. Sonya has 140 beads. How many bags of 10 beads does she need so that she will have 200 beads in all?

_______ bags of beads

2. Choose all the numbers that have the digit 8 in the tens place.

   - ○ 148
   - ○ 387
   - ○ 836
   - ○ 881

3. Draw 139 using hundred boxes, ten sticks, and circles. Write the number name. Then write the number in expanded form.

GO ON

Name ____

4. Robin has 180 stickers. How many pages of 10 stickers does she need so that she will have 200 stickers in all?

______ pages of stickers

---

5. Choose all the numbers that have the digit 2 in the tens place.

- ○ 721
- ○ 142
- ○ 425
- ○ 239

---

6. Count the hundreds, tens, and ones. Write the total.

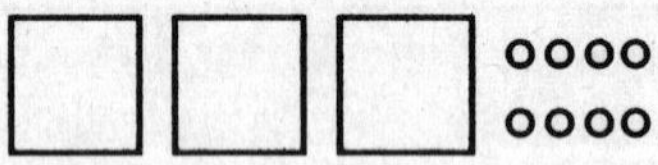

__________ __________ __________ Total __________

Hundreds Tens Ones

Name ________________________________

Learning Objective
Show that 100, 200, 300, 400, 500, 600, 700, 800, and 900 refer to a certain number of hundreds.

1.

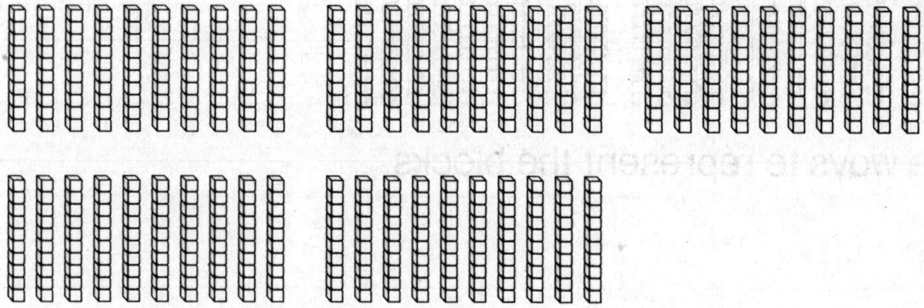

Choose all the ways to represent the blocks.

- ○ 50 hundreds
- ○ 50 tens
- ○ 5 hundreds
- ○ 5 tens

---

2. Pencils are sold in boxes of 10 pencils.
Mr. Lee needs 100 pencils. He has 40 pencils.
How many boxes of 10 pencils should he buy?

______ boxes of 10 pencils

Draw a picture to explain your answer.

GO ON

Name ______________________________

3. 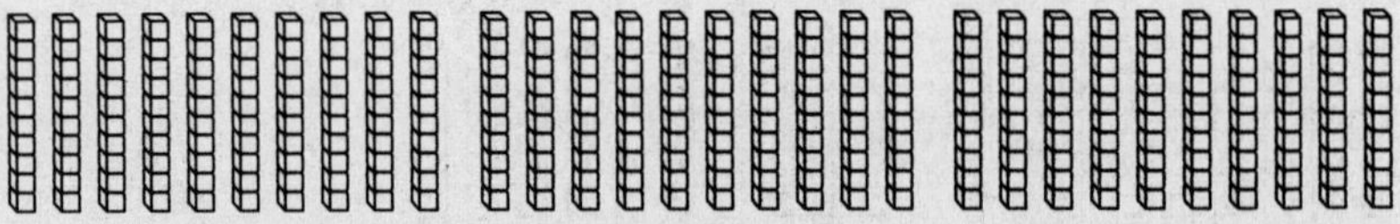

Choose all the ways to represent the blocks.

- ○ 3 hundreds
- ○ 30 ones
- ○ 30 hundreds
- ○ 30 tens

---

4. Write how many tens. Write how many hundreds.
Write the number.

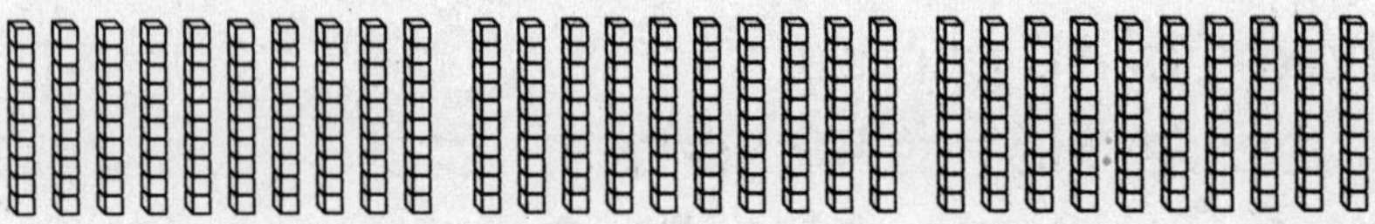

_____ tens

_____ hundreds

_____

---

5. Write how many tens. Write how many hundreds.
Write the number.

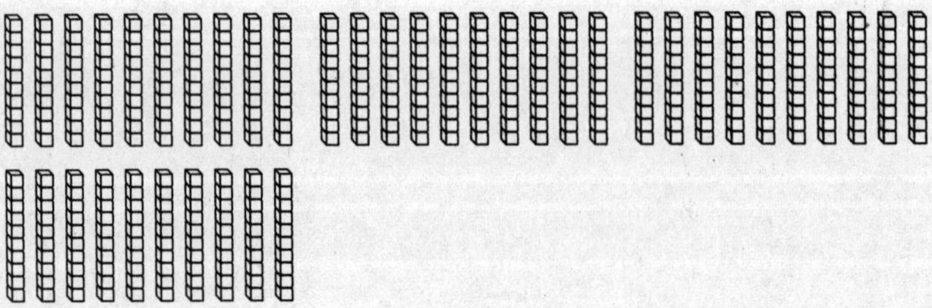

_____ tens

_____ hundreds

_____

STOP

Name ______________________________

Practice Test

Learning Objective
Skip count within 1,000 by 5s, 10s, and 100s.

1. Jen starts at 280 and counts by tens.
   What are the next 6 numbers Jen will say?

   280, ______, ______, ______, ______, ______, ______

---

2. Skip count by 5s.

   35 ______ ______ ______ ______ ______ 65

---

3. Write the numbers that complete each counting pattern.

   25, ______, 35, 40, 45

   10, 20, 30, ______, 50

   50, 60, 70, 80, ______

   70, 75, ______, 85, 90

GO ON

Name ____________________

4. Jeff starts at 190 and counts by tens. What are the next 6 numbers Jeff will say?

190, ______, ______, ______, ______, ______, ______

5. Choose the ways that show counting by tens.

- ○ 550 560 570 580 590 600 610 620 630
- ○ 200 300 400 500 600 700 800 900 1,000
- ○ 650 651 652 653 654 655 656 657 658
- ○ 210 220 230 240 250 260 270 280 290
- ○ 170 180 190 200 210 220 230 240 250

6. Choose the counting pattern that shows counting by fives.

- ○ 76, 77, 78, 79, 80
- ○ 20, 30, 40, 50, 60
- ○ 70, 75, 80, 85, 90
- ○ 40, 42, 44, 46, 48

STOP

Name ____________________

Practice Test

Learning Objective
Read and write numbers to 1,000 using numerals, number names, and expanded form.

1. What is the value of the digit 1 in the number 41?

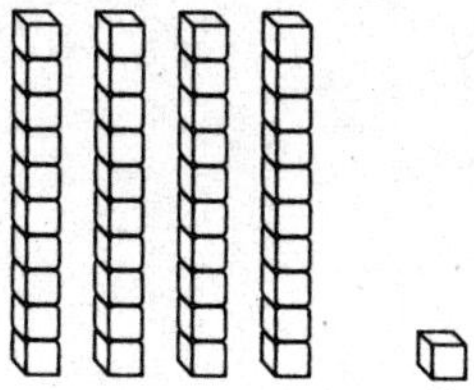

____

2. Draw a picture to show the number 52.

Describe the number 52 in two ways.

2 5	tens	2 5	ones

_______ + _______

3. Dan has a favorite number. His number has the digit 8 in the ones place and the digit 5 in the tens place. What is Dan's favorite number?

____

GO ON

Name ___________________________________

4. It's 154 days until Jeff's birthday. Write the number of days in words.

____

Show the number in two other ways.

Hundreds	Tens	Ones

_____ + _____ + _____

5. Straws are sold in boxes, in bags, or as single straws. Each box has 10 bags in it. Each bag has 10 straws in it. Mr. Tan needs 355 straws. Draw a picture to show a way to buy 355 straws.

How many boxes, bags, and single straws did you show?

____

____

6. Terry has 164 marbles.

Write the number in words.

STOP

____

Name ______________________________

Practice Test

Learning Objective
Compare two three-digit numbers using >, =, or <.

1. Fill in the bubble next to all the comparisons that are true.

   ○ 343 < 328

   ○ 705 > 699

   ○ 691 > 706

   ○ 115 < 120

---

2. Jill and Ed collect postcards. Jill has 124 postcards. Ed has 131 postcards. Who has more postcards? ________

   Jill gets 10 more postcards. Ed gets 5 more postcards. Who has more postcards now? ________

   Draw quick pictures to show how many postcards Jill and Ed have now.

Jill's postcards	Ed's postcards

---

3. Write a symbol from a tile to compare numbers.

   < = >

   143 ◯ 143

GO ON

Name ______________________

4. Write the symbols that make each comparison true. Choose $>$, $<$, or $=$.

787 ______ 769

405 ______ 399

396 ______ 402

128 ______ 131

---

5. Dan and Hannah collect toy cars. Dan has 132 cars. Hannah has 138 cars. Who has more cars? ______

Dan gets 10 more cars. Hannah gets 3 more cars. Who has more cars now? ______

Draw quick pictures to show how many cars Dan and Hannah have now.

Dan's Cars	Hannah's Cars

---

6. Match the pairs of numbers to $=$, $<$, or $>$.

183 ◯ 138 • • $=$

182 ◯ 208 • • $<$

947 ◯ 947 • • $>$

STOP

Name ______________________________

Practice Test

Learning Objective
Add and subtract fluently within 100 using strategies based on place value and/or the relationship between addition and subtraction.

1. Without finding the sums, choose all the pairs of addends that have sums greater than 100.

- ○ 77 + 12
- ○ 49 + 72
- ○ 16 + 95
- ○ 47 + 46

Explain how you decided which pairs have a sum greater than 100.

____

____

2. Which pair of numbers do you need to regroup to subtract?

- ○ 55 − 24
- ○ 39 − 18
- ○ 30 − 19
- ○ 73 − 63

3. Use the number line. Count up to find the difference.

53 − 46 = ______

GO ON

Name ______________________________

4. What is 46 − 28? Use the numbers on the tiles to rewrite the subtraction problem. Then find the difference.

18	28	46	74

☐
− ☐
———
☐

Regroup if you need to. Write the difference.

5.

Tens	Ones
☐	☐
4	6
− 1	9

6.

Tens	Ones
☐	☐
7	5
− 2	5

7. Subtract 18 from 35. Draw to show the regrouping. Fill in the bubbles next to all the ways to write the difference.

- ○ 7 tens 1 one
- ○ 17
- ○ 1 ten 7 ones
- ○ 71

STOP

Name ____________________

Practice Test

Learning Objective
Add up to four two-digit numbers using strategies based on place value and properties of operations.

1. There are 18 girls in the chorus. There are 9 boys. How many children are there in the chorus?

   Draw quick pictures to solve. Write the sum.

Tens	Ones

_____ children

Did you regroup to find the answer? Explain.

____

____

2. On four days of this week, Madelyn practiced her violin 43 minutes, 32 minutes, 16 minutes, and 25 minutes.

   Write a number sentence to show the number of minutes Madelyn practiced her violin.

____

3. Olivia sees 16 crabs at the beach. Then she sees 7 more. Choose all the ways you can use to find how many crabs Olivia sees.

   ○ 16 − 7

   ○ 16 + 7

   ○ 16 + 4 + 3

GO ON

Name ______________________________

4. Lauren sees 14 birds. Her friend sees 7 birds. How many birds do Lauren and her friend see? Draw quick pictures to solve. Write the sum.

Tens	Ones

______ birds

Did you regroup to find the answer? Explain.

____

____

5. Leah put 21 white marbles, 31 black marbles, and 7 blue marbles in a bag. Then her sister added 19 yellow marbles.

Write a number sentence to show the number of marbles in the bag.

____

6. Leslie finds 24 paper clips in her desk. She finds 8 more paper clips in her pencil box. Choose all the ways you can use to find how many paper clips Leslie has in all.

- ○ $24 + 8$
- ○ $24 - 8$
- ○ $24 + 6 + 2$

STOP

Name ____

Practice Test

Learning Objective
Add and subtract within 1,000, using strategies based on place value, properties of operations, and/or the relationship between addition and subtraction.

1. At the store, there are 863 rocks and shells. There are 121 rocks. How many shells are there? Circle the number that makes the sentence true.

There are [642 / 732 / 742] shells.

2. A bird watcher counted 163 white birds and 185 black birds. How many birds did she count?

$$\begin{array}{r} 163 \\ +\ 185 \\ \hline \end{array} \longrightarrow \begin{array}{r} 100 + 60 + 3 \\ +\ 100 + 80 + 5 \\ \hline \end{array}$$

Select one number from each column to solve the problem.

Hundreds	Tens	Ones
○ 2	○ 4	○ 6
○ 3	○ 5	○ 7
○ 4	○ 6	○ 8

GO ON

Name ____

3. A farmer has 305 sheep. She moves 263 sheep into a field.

Choose all the sentences that describe how to find how many sheep are left.

- ○ Regroup 1 hundred as 10 tens.
- ○ Regroup 1 ten as 10 ones.
- ○ Subtract 6 tens from 10 tens.

---

4. Use the numbers on the tiles to solve the problem.

3	5	7

$$\begin{array}{r} 2\;9\;9 \\ +\;2\;3\;\square \\ \hline \square\;\square\;6 \end{array}$$

Describe how you solved the problem.

____

____

____

____

STOP

Name ____________________

Learning Objective
Add 10 or 100 to or subtract 10 or 100 from a given number mentally (up to 900).

1. A store has 263 board games. It has 100 fewer puzzles than board games. The store has 10 more action figures than puzzles. Write the number of each.

______ board games ______ puzzles ______ action figures

---

2. Write the next number in each counting pattern.

162, 262, 362, 462, ______

347, 357, 367, 377, ______

609, 619, 629, 639, ______

---

3. Use the clues to answer the question.

- Shawn counts 213 cars.
- Maria counts 100 fewer cars than Shawn.
- Jayden counts 10 more cars than Maria.

How many cars does Jayden count? ______ cars

GO ON

Name ____________________

4. Sanjo has 348 marbles. Harry has 100 fewer marbles than Sanjo. Ari has 10 more marbles than Harry. Write the number of marbles each child has.

________ ________ ________

Sanjo Ari Harry

5. Rick has 10 more crayons than Lori. Lori has 136 crayons. Tom has 10 fewer crayons than Rick. How many crayons does each child have?

Rick: ________ crayons

Tom: ________ crayons

Lori: ________ crayons

6. Rico has 235 stickers. Gabby has 100 more stickers than Rico. Thomas has 10 fewer stickers than Gabby. Write the number of stickers each child has.

________ ________ ________

Rico Gabby Thomas

STOP

Name ______________________

Practice Test

Learning Objective
Show that addition and subtraction strategies work using place value and properties of operations.

1. Draw a quick picture to solve. Write the difference.

	Tens	Ones
	☐	☐
	8	1
−	5	6

Tens	Ones

Explain what you did to find the difference.

____

____

____

2. Diana has 196 marbles. She gives away 42 of her marbles to her sister. What step should Diana follow first to find out how many marbles she has now?

○ Ungroup 6 tens as 5 tens 10 ones.

○ Subtract 2 ones from 9 tens.

○ Subtract 2 ones from 6 ones.

○ Subtract 4 ones from 9 tens.

GO ON

Name ____________________

3. Subtract 46 from 73. Explain all the steps you use.

$$\begin{array}{r} 73 \\ -46 \\ \hline \end{array}$$

---

4. Draw a quick picture to solve. Write the difference.

	Tens	Ones
	☐	☐
	6	2
−	2	5

Tens	Ones

Explain what you did to find the difference.

____

____

____

STOP

Name ______________________________

Practice Test

Learning Objective
Measure the length of an object by selecting and using appropriate tools.

1. Owen wants to measure the length of a chalkboard.

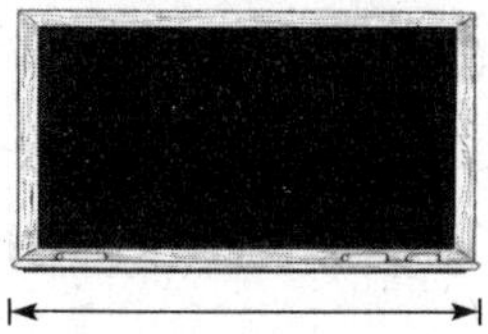

Circle the best choice of tool.

tiles	inch ruler	yardstick

Explain your choice of tool.

____

____

2. Zach uses tiles to measure a straw. Each tile is 1 inch long. Zach says the straw is 4 inches long. Is he correct? Explain.

____

____

GO ON

Name ________________________________

3. Josh wants to measures the distance around a soccer ball.

Circle the best choice of tool.

inch ruler yardstick measuring tape

Explain your choice of tool.

____

____

4. Measure the length of the paintbrush to the nearest centimeter. Circle the number in the box that makes the sentence true.

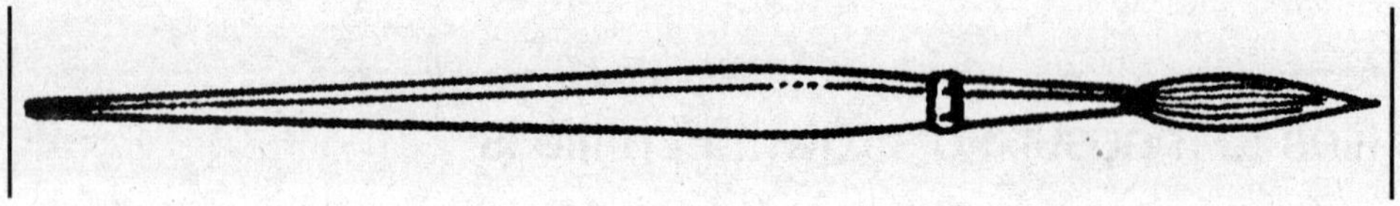

The paintbrush is about [12 / 13 / 15] centimeters long.

STOP

Name ______________________________

Practice Test

Learning Objective
Measure the length of an object twice using two different length units.

1. Write the word that makes the sentence true.

centimeters	meters

A pencil is 16 ____________ long.

A swimming pool is 50 ____________ long.

A sidewalk is 2 ____________ wide.

A computer keyboard is 42 ____________ wide.

---

2. Use an inch ruler. What is the length of the string to the nearest inch?

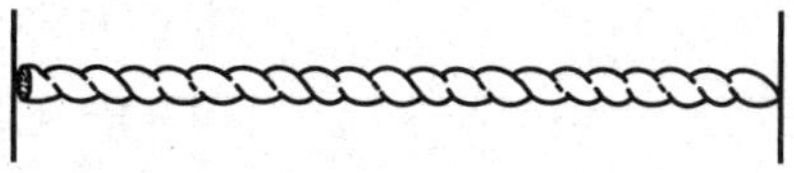

Circle the number in the box to make the sentence true.

The string is [2 / 3 / 4] inches long.

GO ON

Name ______________________________

3. Measure the crayon in centimeters and in inches.

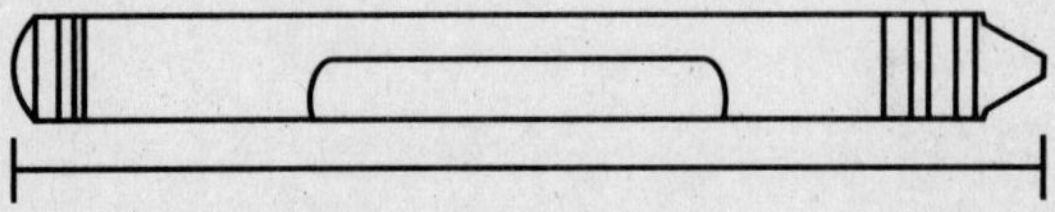

Circle the number or words in each box that makes the sentence true.

<table><tr><td>The crayon is</td><td>6
7
8</td><td>centimeters long.</td></tr></table>

<table><tr><td>The crayon is about</td><td>1
2
3</td><td>inches long.</td></tr></table>

<table><tr><td>There are more</td><td>inches than centimeters

centimeters than inches</td><td>because</td><td>inches are smaller than centimeters.

centimeters are smaller than inches.</td></tr></table>

STOP

Name ____________________

1. The paintbrush is about 7 centimeters long.
Gavin says the feather is about 8 centimeters long.
Ray says the feather is about 5 centimeters long.

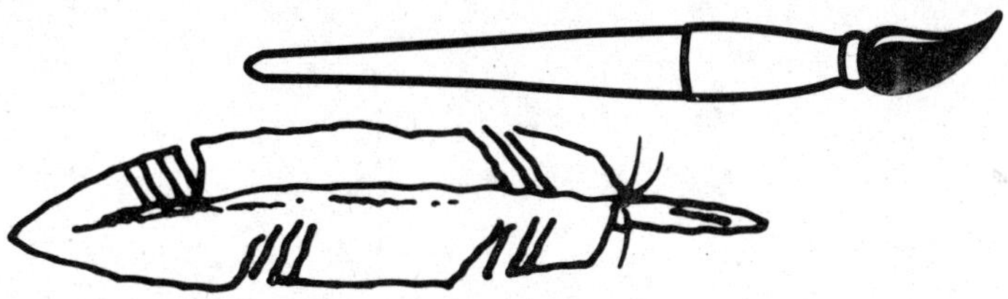

Which boy has the better estimate? Explain.

____

____

____

---

2. Ella lays 1-inch tiles in a line until the line has the same length as a football.

Which sentence best estimates the length of a football?

- ○ A football is less than 6 tiles long.
- ○ A football is about 12 tiles long.
- ○ A football is more than 6 feet long.
- ○ A football is more than 50 tiles long.

GO ON

Name ______________________________

3. The paper clip is about 4 centimeters long. Robin says the string is about 7 centimeters long. Gale says the string is about 20 centimeters long.

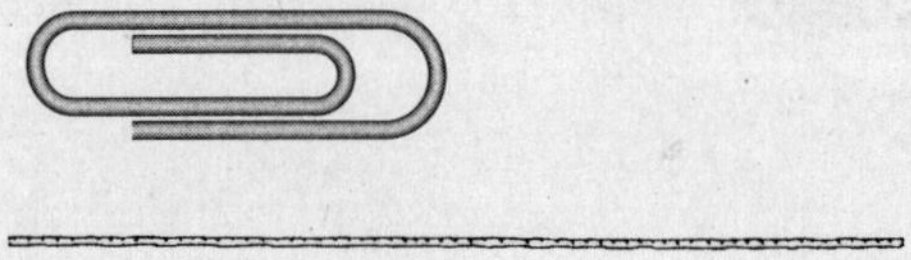

Which girl has the better estimate? Explain.

____

____

---

4. Estimate the length of a real horse. Fill in the bubble next to all the sentences that are true.

○ The horse is less than 1 meter long.

○ The horse is less than 6 meters long.

○ The horse is more than 3 centimeters long.

○ The horse is about 6 centimeters long.

○ The horse is about 3 meters long.

STOP

Learning Objective
Measure to find how much longer one object is than another, and use a standard length unit to express that difference.

Name ______________________________

1. Alberto uses 8 centimeters of wire for a science project. He uses another 15 centimeters of wire for another project. How many centimeters of wire does he use?

   Draw a diagram. Write a number sentence using a ■ for the missing number. Then solve.

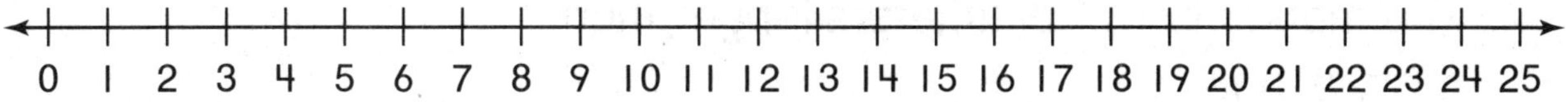

____

Alberto uses ______ centimeters of wire.

---

2. Measure the length of each object. Choose all the sentences that describe the objects.

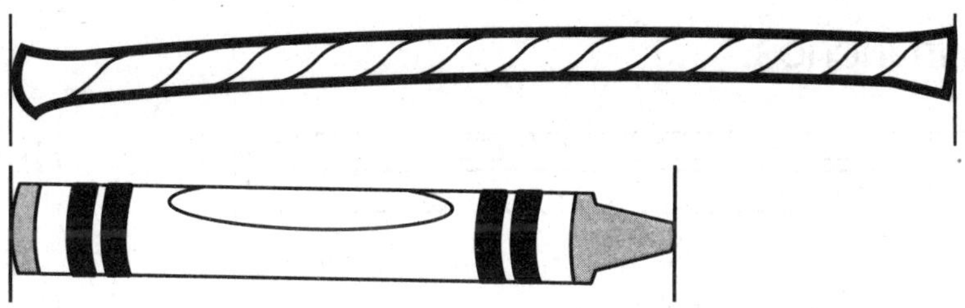

______ centimeters

______ centimeters

○ The yarn is 3 centimeters longer than the crayon.

○ The crayon is 7 centimeters shorter than the yarn.

○ The total length of the yarn and the crayon is 17 centimeters.

GO ON

Name ______________________________

3. Measure the length of each object. Choose all the sentences that describe the objects.

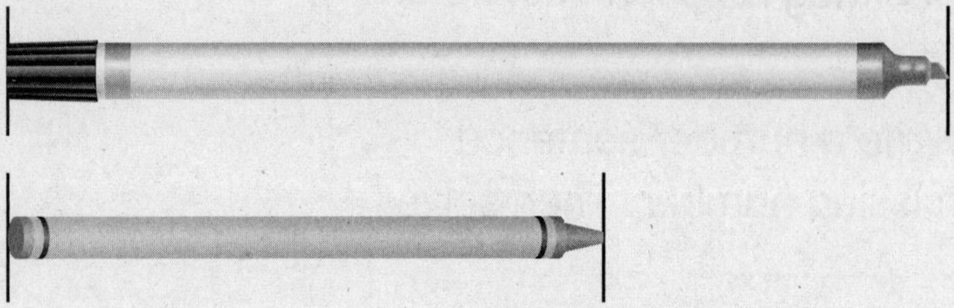

______ centimeters

______ centimeters

○ The marker is 11 centimeters longer than the crayon.

○ The crayon is 4 centimeters shorter than the marker.

○ The total length of the marker and the crayon is 18 centimeters.

---

4. Measure each pencil in inches.

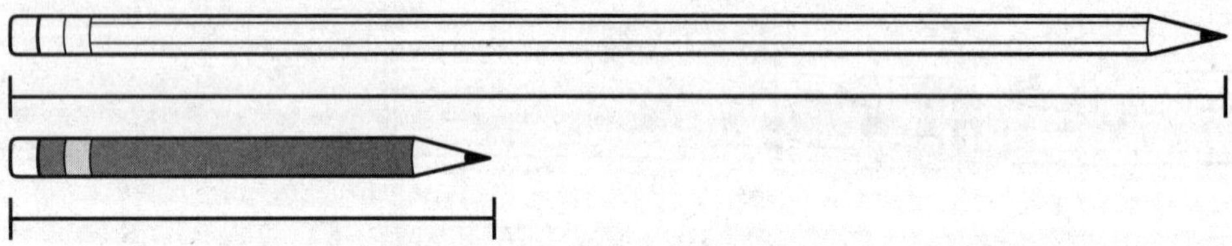

☐ inches

☐ inches

Which sentence is true?

○ The gray pencil is 4 inches longer than the white pencil.

○ The white pencil is 6 inches longer than the gray pencil.

○ The white pencil is 4 inches longer than the gray pencil.

STOP

Name ______________________________

Practice Test

Learning Objective
Add or subtract within 100 to solve word problems involving lengths by using drawings and equations.

1. Meg has a ribbon that is 9 inches long. She has another ribbon that is 11 inches long. How many inches of ribbon does Meg have?

Draw a diagram. Write a number sentence using a ■ for the missing number. Solve.

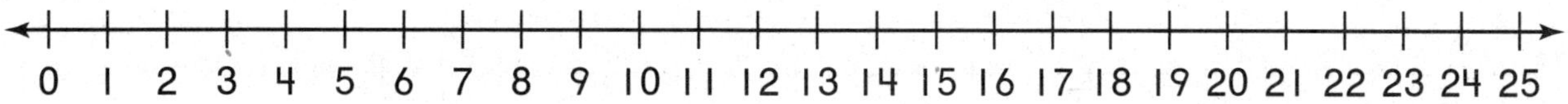

____

Meg has ______ inches of ribbon.

---

2. Michael has 54 centimeters of brown ribbon. He has 16 more centimeters of yellow ribbon than brown ribbon. How many centimeters of yellow ribbon does Michael have?

Michael has [38 / 60 / 70] centimeters of yellow ribbon.

---

3. Margaret wants to build a block tower 80 inches tall. So far her tower is 22 inches tall. How much taller does Margaret need to build her tower?

Margaret needs to build her tower [52 / 58 / 102] inches taller.

GO ON

Name ______________________________

4. Luke has a string that is 6 inches long and a string that is 11 inches long. How many inches of string does Luke have?

Draw a diagram. Write a number sentence using a ■ for the missing number. Solve.

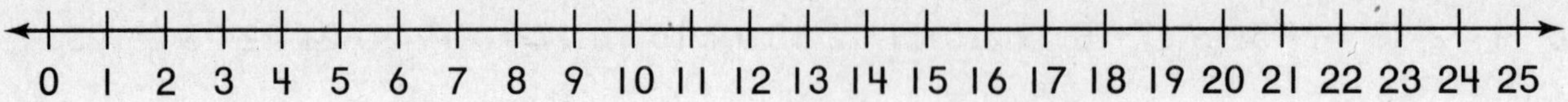

____

Luke has ______ inches of string.

Write an equation and solve.

5. Mrs. Samson puts a fence around her patio. The patio has three sides. One side is 14 feet long. The second side is 17 feet long. The third side is 9 feet long. How many feet of fencing does Mrs. Samson use?

______________ = ☐ ______________
unit

---

6. Olivia puts lace around the outside of a square pillow. Each side of the pillow is 18 centimeters long. How many centimeters of lace does Olivia need?

______________ = ☐ ______________
unit

STOP

Name ______________________________

Practice Test

Learning Objective
Represent whole number sums and differences within 100 on a number line.

1. Elizabeth has a piece of ribbon that is 25 centimeters long. She cuts off a piece of the ribbon to use to wrap a gift. Elizabeth's ribbon is now 7 centimeters long. How many centimeters of ribbon did Elizabeth use to wrap the gift?

   Write a number sentence using a ■ for the missing number. Then solve.

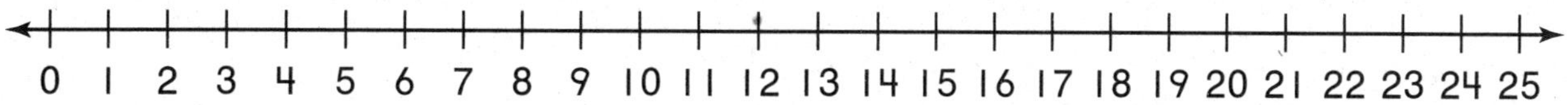

____

Elizabeth used ______ centimeters of ribbon.

---

2. Complete the equation that the number line diagram represents.

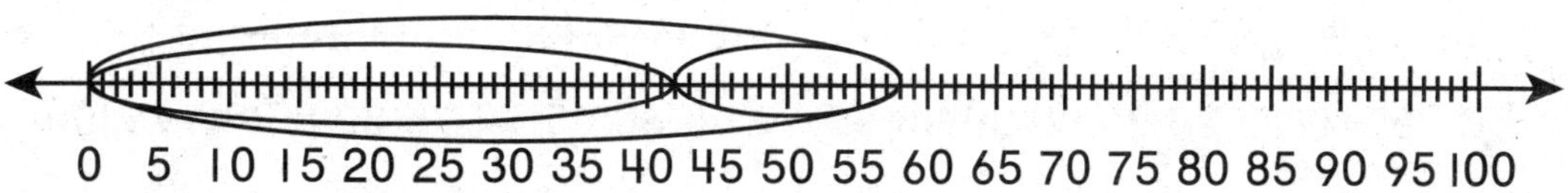

□ + 16 = □

GO ON

Name ______________________________

3. Ethan's rope is 25 centimeters long. Ethan cuts the rope and gives a piece to Hank. Ethan's rope is now 16 centimeters long. How many centimeters of rope does Hank have?

Draw a diagram. Write a number sentence using a ▒ for the missing number. Then solve.

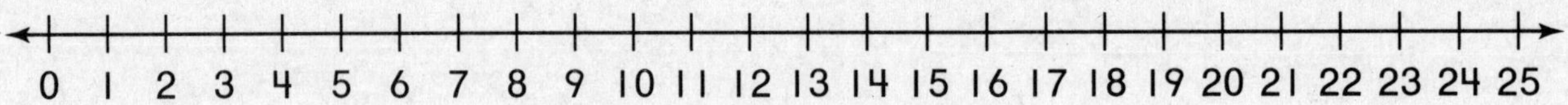

____

Hank has ________ centimeters of rope.

4. Represent the equation on the number line diagram.

47 + ▒ = 68

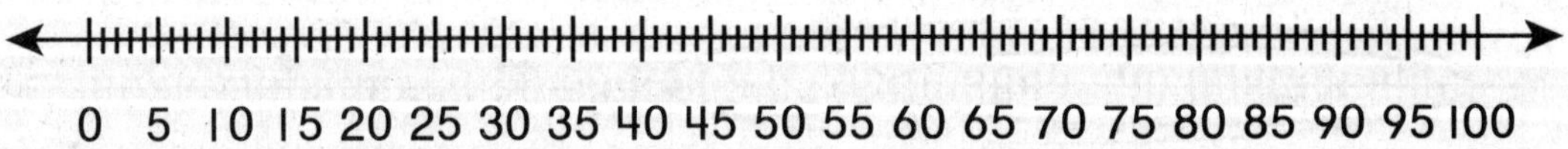

Find the difference.

47 + ☐ = 68

Name ______________________

Practice Test

Learning Objective
Tell and write time to the nearest 5 minutes, with a.m. and p.m., using analog clocks.

1. The clock shows the time Sarah starts getting ready for bed. Write the time. Circle A.M. or P.M.

A.M.

____

P.M.

Tell how you knew whether to select A.M. or P.M.

____

____

2. Write the times the clocks show.

__________ __________ __________

GO ON

Name ____

3. Write the times the clocks show.

__________ __________ __________

4. Write the times the clocks show.

__________ __________ __________

5. What time is shown on the clock? Fill in the bubbles next to all the ways to write or say the time.

- ○ 3:45
- ○ 9:15
- ○ 15 minutes past 9
- ○ half past 9

STOP

Name ______________________________

1. Ben has 30¢. Circle coins to show this amount.

2. Marta pays $1.80 for a snack.

Fill in the bubble next to all the ways that show $1.80.

○ one $1 bill, 2 quarters, and 3 dimes

○ one $1 bill, 3 quarters, and 1 nickel

○ 5 quarters and 3 dimes

○ 7 quarters and 1 nickel

3. Antoine gave Fran these coins. Antoine says he gave Fran $1.00. Is Antoine correct? Explain.

____

____

GO ON

Name ________________________________

4. James paid for a drink with this money.

Circle the amount to complete the sentence.

James paid a total of [$1.41 / $1.46 / $1.61] for the drink.

---

5. Hannah gave her sister these coins. Write the value of the coins. Explain how you found the total value.

____

____

---

6. Kim has 60¢. Circle coins to show this amount.

STOP

Name ______________________________

Practice Test

Learning Objective
Generate measurement data by finding lengths of objects to the nearest whole unit, and show measurements using a line plot.

1. Drew made a line plot to show the lengths of his toy boats. How many boats are shown in the line plot?

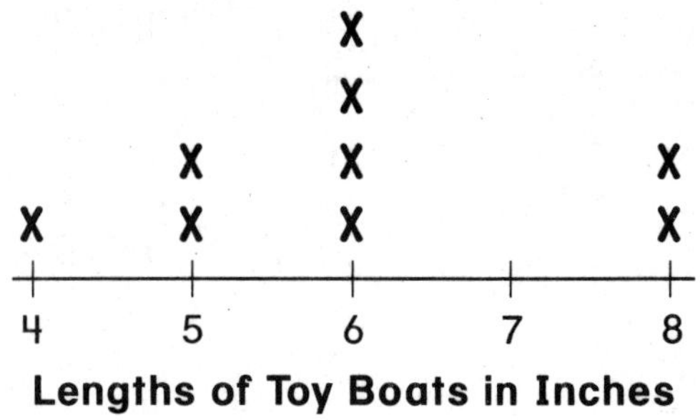

The line plot shows ______ toy boats.

Suppose one of the toy boats that is 5 inches long breaks and is thrown away. Explain how Drew should change the line plot.

____

2. Dalia made a line plot to show the lengths of her ribbons. How many ribbons are shown in the line plot?

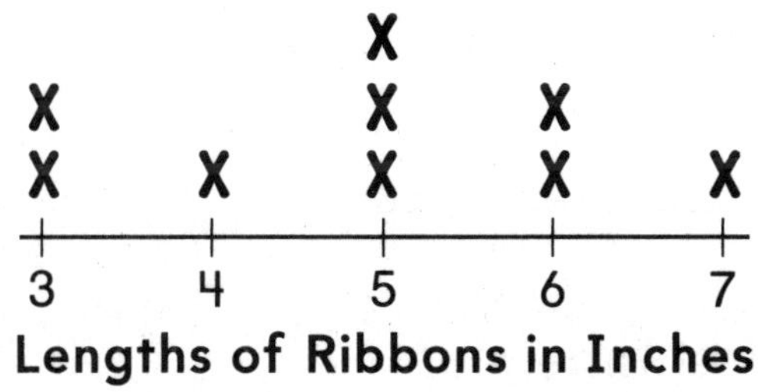

The line plot shows ______ ribbons.

Suppose Dalia cut one of the ribbons that is 6 inches long into two pieces that are each 3 inches long. Explain how she should change the line plot.

____

____

GO ON

Name ______________________________

3. Measure each string to the nearest centimeter. Then match the string to its length.

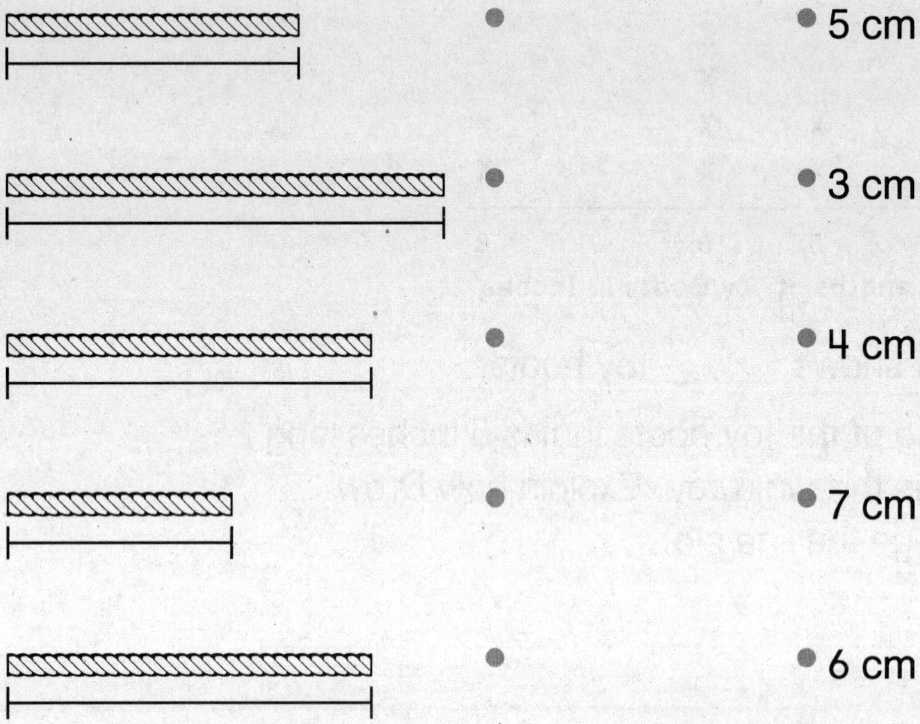

---

4. Show the lengths of the five strings in question 3 on this line plot.

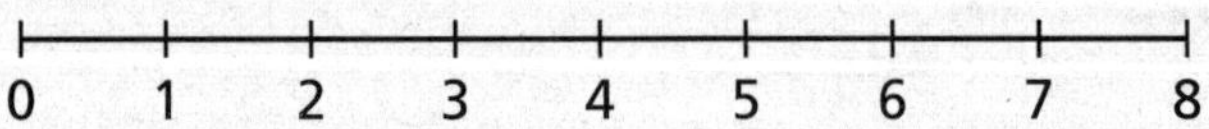

Lengths of Strings (centimeters)

How many strings are longer than 4 cm?

☐ strings

STOP

Name ______________________________

Practice Test

Learning Objective
Draw a bar graph and a picture graph to represent a data set with up to four categories.

1. Use the tally chart to complete the picture graph. Draw a ☺ for each child.

Favorite School Subject	
math	||||
reading	|||
science	||
art	|||

Favorite School Subject					
math					
reading					
science					
art					

Key: Each ☺ stands for 1 child.

2. How many children chose art?

_____ children

3. How many more children chose math than science?

_____ more children

4. Name two subjects that were chosen by a total of 6 children.

____

GO ON

Name ______________________________

5. Eric asked some friends to name their favorite sandwiches. Use the data to complete the bar graph.

4 children like ham.

6 children like turkey.

1 child likes cheese.

3 children like jelly.

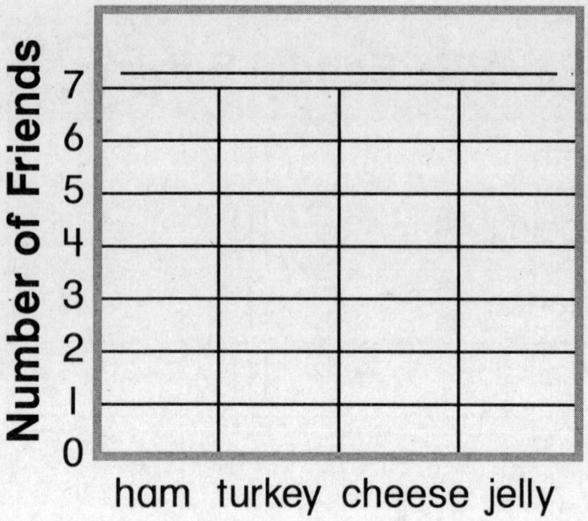

6. Fill in the bubble next to all the sentences that describe the data in the bar graph above.

○ 6 children chose ham.

○ Turkey was the most popular.

○ 7 children chose cheese or jelly.

○ 5 more children chose turkey than cheese.

7. Did more children choose cheese or jelly than ham? Explain.

____

____

8. How many children chose a sandwich other than turkey?

_____ children

STOP

Name ______________________________

Practice Test

Learning Objective
Identify and draw shapes having specified attributes.

1. Match the shapes.

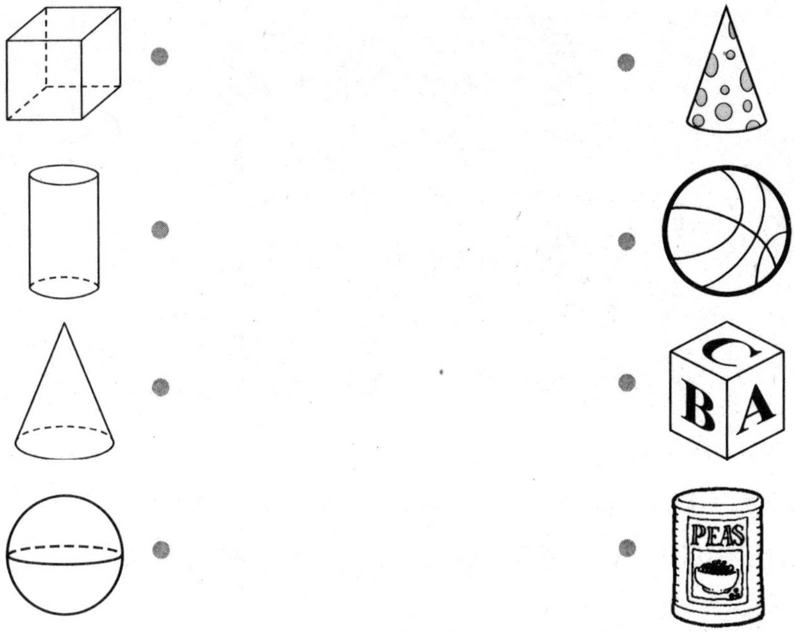

---

2. Write the numbers that make each sentence true.

A rectangular prism has ______ faces.

Each face of a rectangular prism has ______ edges.

A rectangular prism has ______ vertices.

A rectangular prism has ______ edges.

GO ON

Name ______________________________

3. Alex built this rectangular prism. Circle the number of unit cubes Alex used.

4. Paul makes a hexagon and a triangle with straws. He uses one straw for each side of a shape. How many straws does Paul need?

______ straws

5. Draw each shape where it belongs in the chart.

Shapes with 4 or Fewer Angles	Shapes with More than 4 Angles

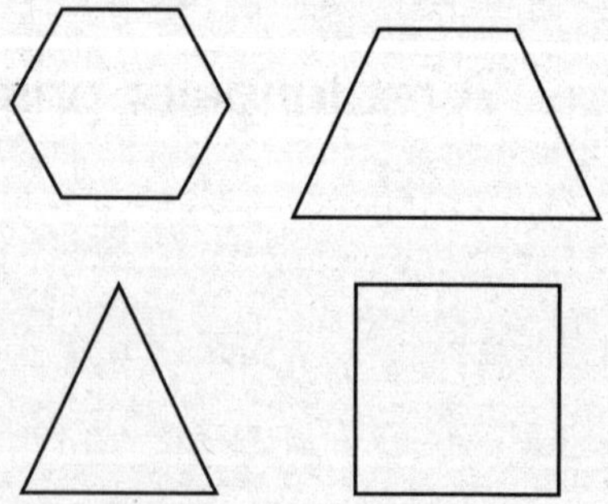

STOP

Practice Test

Learning Objective
Partition a rectangle into same-size squares, and count to find the total number of squares.

Name ______________________________

1. Max wants to cover the rectangle with gray tiles. Explain how you would estimate the number of gray tiles he would need to cover the rectangle.

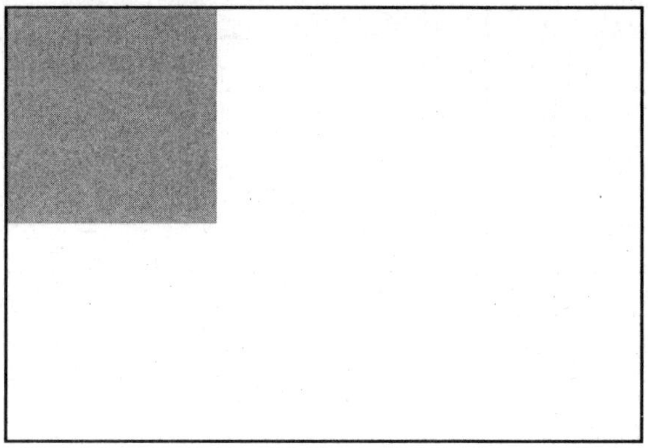

____

____

2. Measure in centimeters. Draw rows and columns. Write the number of small squares.

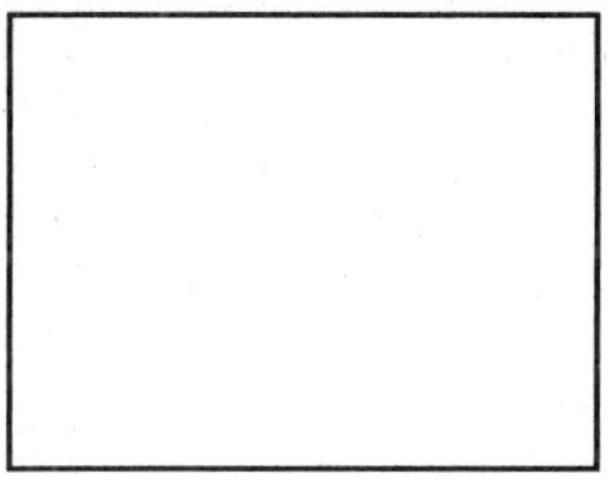

_____ squares

3. Measure in inches. Draw rows and columns. Write the number of small squares.

_____ squares

GO ON

Name ____________________

4. Grace wants to cover the rectangle with gray tiles. Explain how you would estimate the number of gray tiles she would need to cover the rectangle.

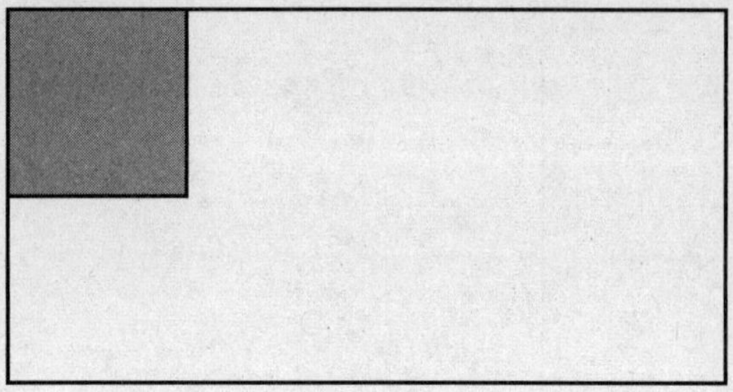

____

____

5. Mary started to cover this rectangle with ones blocks. Explain how you would estimate the number of ones blocks that would cover the whole rectangle.

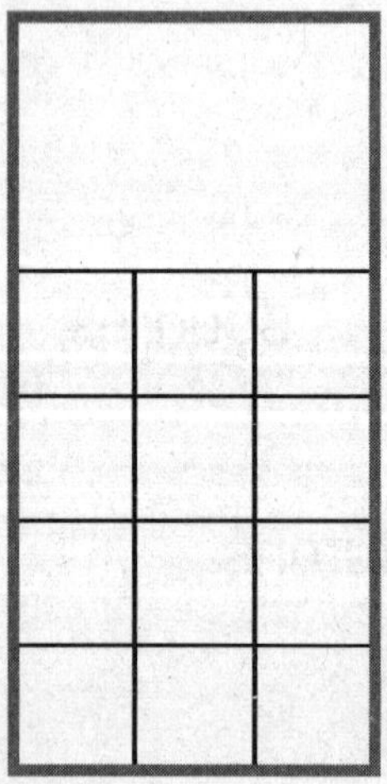

____

____

____

STOP

Learning Objective
Partition circles and rectangles into two, three, or four equal shares, and recognize that equal shares of identical wholes need not have the same shape.

Name ______________________________

1. Draw lines to show fourths.

Explain how you know that the parts are fourths.

____

____

2. Hector makes two equal sized sandwiches. He cuts both sandwiches into thirds. What are two different ways he can cut the sandwiches? Draw to show your answer.

3. Fill in the bubble next to the shapes that show thirds.

○ 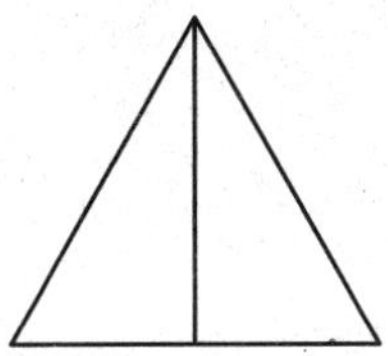

○ 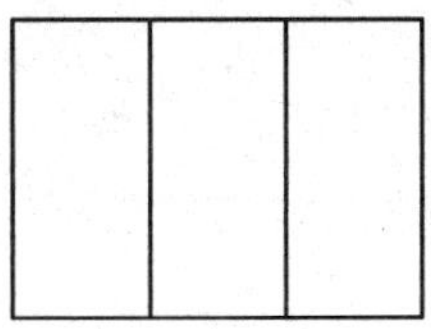

○ 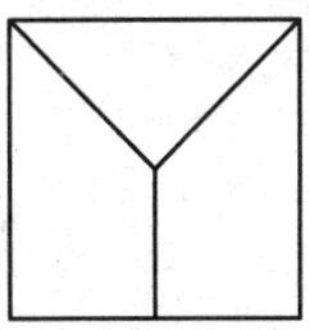

○ 

GO ON

Name ______________________________

4. Draw lines in each shape to make equal shares.

Two Halves	Three Thirds	Four Fourths
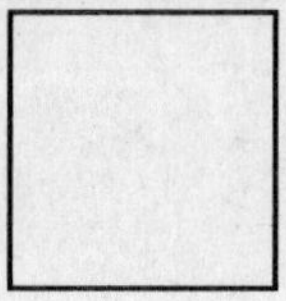	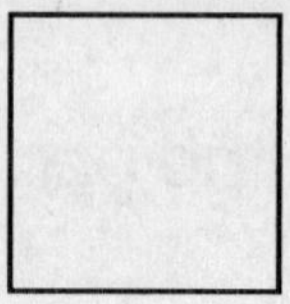	
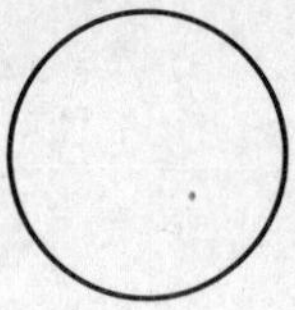	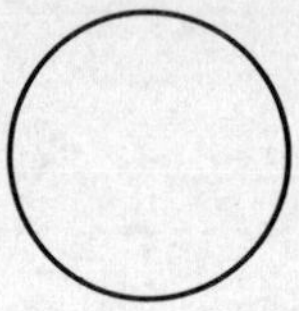	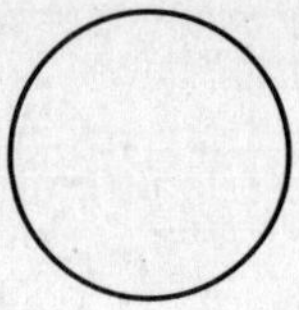

5. Choose the rectangles that show a fourth shaded.

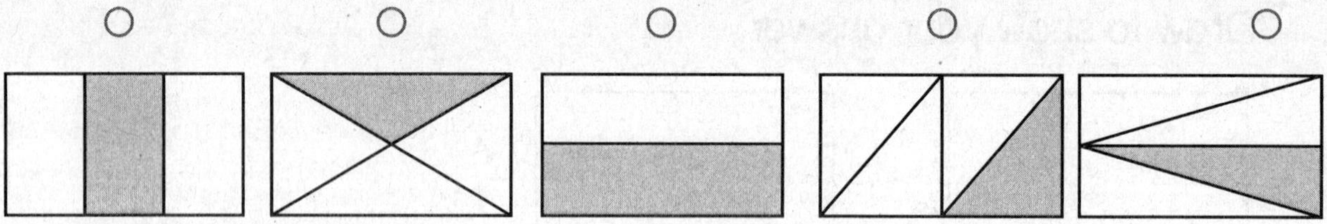

6. Write a term from a tile to tell how much is shaded.

a fourth of	a third of	a half of

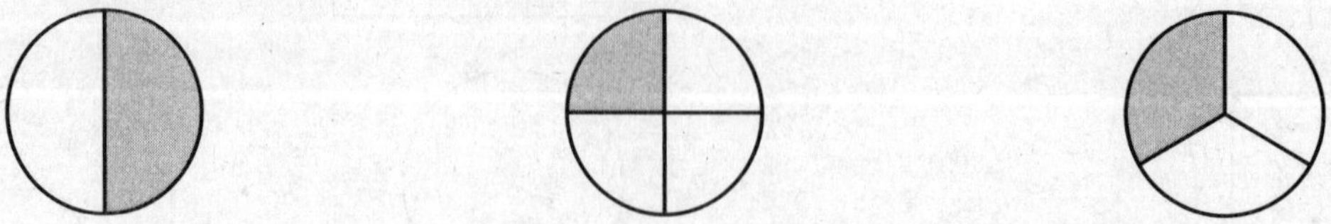

________ ________ ________

STOP

1. Carlos uses 400 − 300 to estimate how many more girls than boys are in a school.

   Fill in the bubble next to all the problems he may have been estimating for.

○	○	○	○
395 − 218	360 − 324	480 − 341	417 − 288

---

2. Complete the equation that the diagram represents.

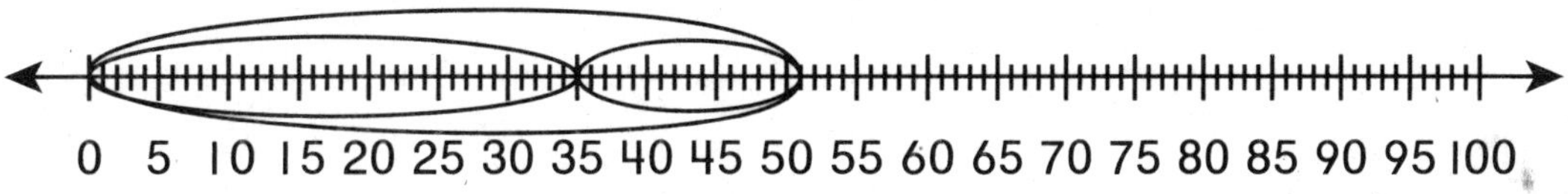

$\square + 16 = \square$

---

3. Use the data in the list to complete the line plot.

Lengths of Ribbons

6 inches
5 inches
7 inches
6 inches

______ ______ ______

____

---

4. Draw to show halves, thirds, and fourths.

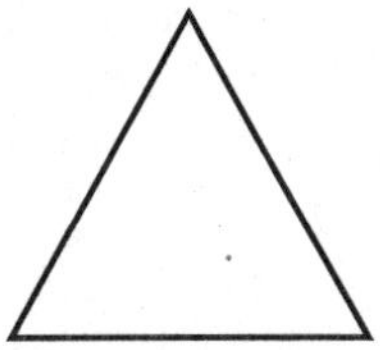

halves

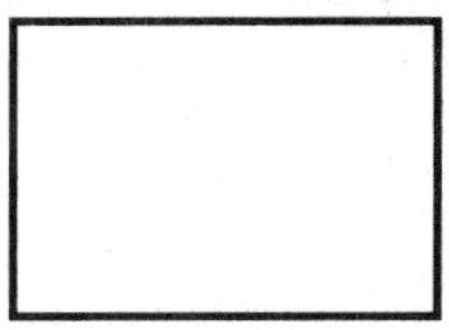

thirds

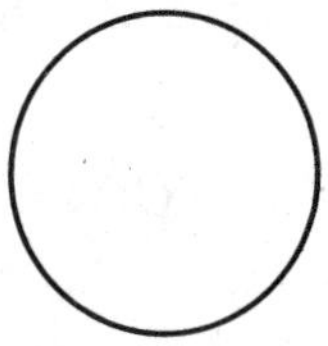

fourths

GO ON

5. Draw and label coins to show a total value of 65¢.

---

6. Tricia has 12 pencils to share equally with her classmate. Draw a picture to show how Tricia can share her pencils.

How many pencils will Tricia keep?

_______ pencils

---

7. Kate sees 4 white dogs, 9 brown dogs, and 3 black dogs at the park. How many dogs does she see at the park?

_______ dogs

---

8. Aya has 167 baseball cards. She gives away 35 of her cards to a friend. Choose which step will help Aya to figure out how many baseball cards she has left.

○ Ungroup 7 tens as 6 tens 10 ones.

○ Subtract 5 ones from 6 tens.

○ Subtract 3 tens from 6 tens.

GO ON

Name ______________________________

9. Use an inch ruler. What is the length of the crayon to the nearest inch?

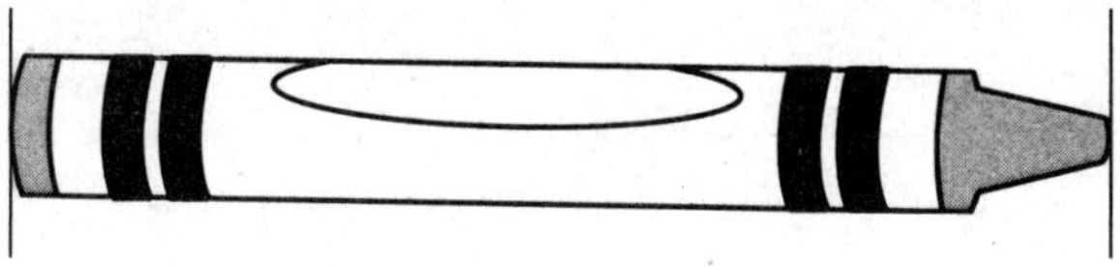

______ inches

10. Use the 1-inch mark. Estimate the length of each piece of yarn.

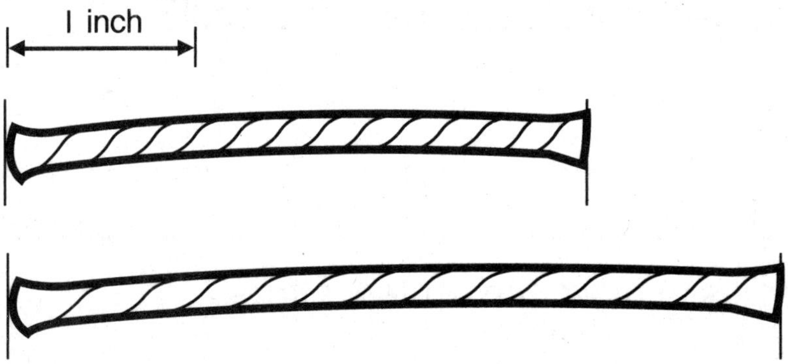

about ______ inches

about ______ inches

11. Measure in centimeters. Draw rows and columns. Write the number of small squares.

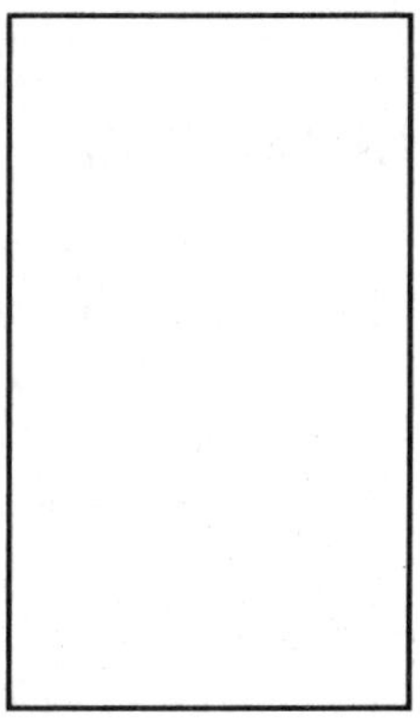

______ squares

GO ON

12. Frank counts by twos to 20. Elsie counts by ones to 10. Who will say more numbers? Explain.

____

____

---

13. Write an equation and solve.

Mr. Quito has a square pool. Each side of the pool is 16 feet long. How many feet is it around the whole pool?

____________________ = ☐ ____________________
unit

---

14. Use the words on the tiles to make the sentence true.

The boy is 40 __________ tall.

The car is 12 __________ long.

The driveway is 35 __________ long.

inches | feet

---

15. Shade in the ten frames to show the number.
Circle **even** or **odd**.

15

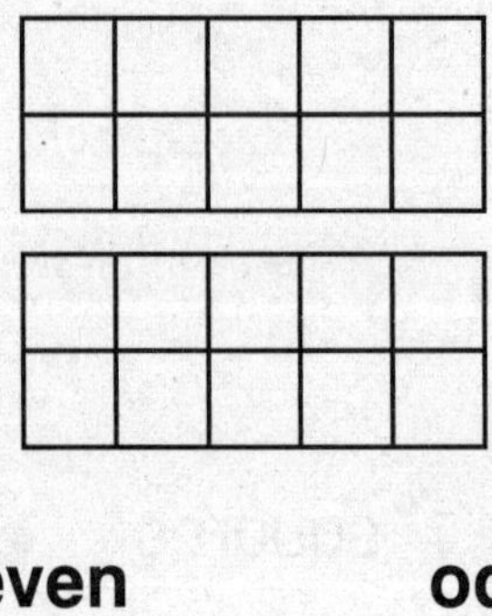

even **odd**

GO ON

16. Andy is thinking of a number that has a digit less than 5 in the tens place. It has a digit greater than 7 in the ones place. Fill in the bubble next to all the numbers that could be Andy's number.

○ 70 + 8

○ forty-nine

○ 2 tens 8 ones

Write another number Andy could be thinking of.

______

---

17. Write a symbol from a tile to compare numbers.

<	=	>

128 ◯ 137

---

18. Find the difference.

$$\begin{array}{r} 70 \\ -\ 38 \\ \hline \end{array}$$

Tens	Ones
○ 2	○ 2
○ 3	○ 3
○ 4	○ 4

GO ON

19. Mason drew 2 two-dimensional shapes that had 8 angles in all. Draw the shapes Mason could have drawn.

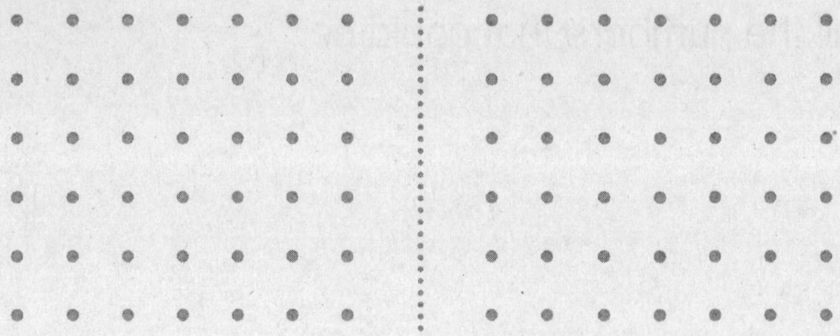

---

20. A store sells 2 boxes of 100 pencils and some single pencils. Choose all the numbers that show how many pencils the store could sell.

○ 219 ○ 206

○ 120 ○ 182

---

21. Dan has 29 animal pictures. Kayla has 37 animal pictures. Who has more animal pictures? How many more? Label the bar model. Solve.

Circle the word or number from each box to make the sentence true.

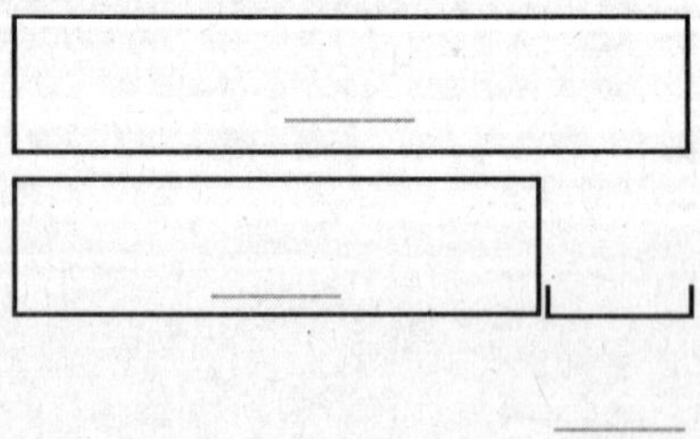

Dan / Kayla	has	22 / 12 / 8	more animal pictures.

GO ON

Name ____________________

22. Write the next number in each counting pattern.

338, 348, 358, 368, ______

472, 572, 672, 772, ______

---

23. Write the time that is shown on this clock.

______ : ______

---

24. Describe how the number of sit-ups that Karina did changed from Monday to Thursday. Make a bar graph to solve the problem.

Monday—1 sit-ups
Tuesday—2 sit-ups
Wednesday—3 sit-ups
Thursday—4 sit-ups

Karina's Sit-Ups

Number of Sit-Ups	Monday	Tuesday	Wednesday	Thursday
4				
3				
2				
1				
0				

Day

____

____

GO ON

25. Write how many tens. Circle groups of 10 tens. Write how many hundreds. Write the number.

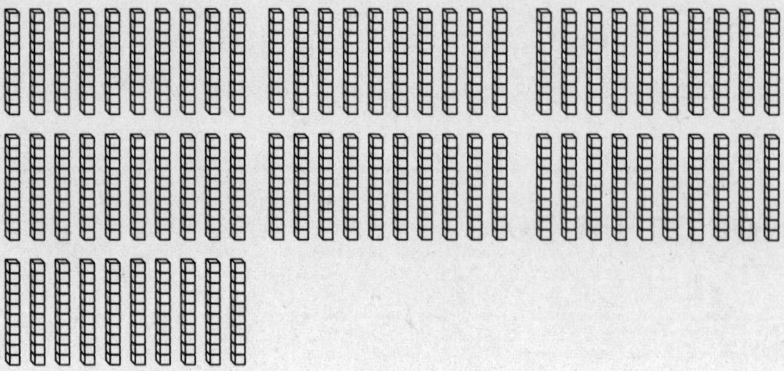

_____ tens

_____ hundreds

_____

---

26. Mandy has 26 baseball cards, 42 football cards, and 38 basketball cards. How many cards does she have?

Mandy has [68 / 80 / 106] cards.

---

27. Measure the length of each object. Complete the number sentence to find the difference between the lengths.

_____ centimeters

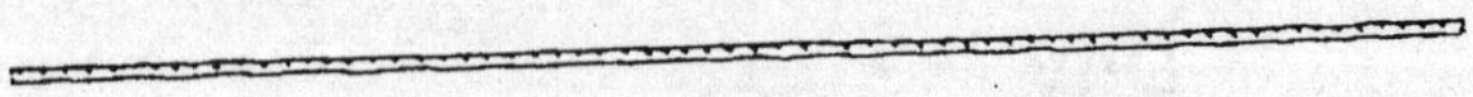

_____ centimeters

_______ – _______ = _______

The string is _____ centimeters longer than the straw.

GO ON

Name ______________________

Two Schools

Jefferson School has students in 1st grade to 5th grade.

1. The number of children in 1st grade has 3 digits.
The digits in the number are 2, 3, and 8.
The digit 8 means 80 in this number.
Write a number that could be the number of children in 1st grade.

---

2. Write a number that is 10 less than the number of children you chose for 1st grade.

---

3. Write a number sentence that uses >, <, or = to compare your answers from questions 1 and 2.

_______ ◯ _______

GO ON

Name ____________________

4. Donell uses these blocks to show the number of students in 3rd grade.

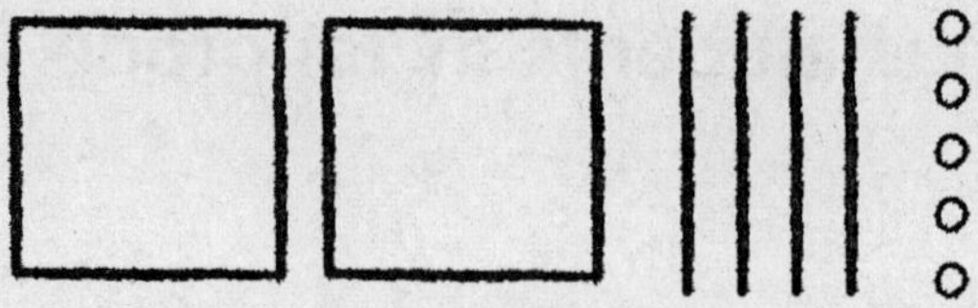

How many students are in 3rd grade?

________ students

---

5. There are 100 more students in 4th grade than in 5th grade. Grade 5 has 176 students. Draw a quick picture to show how many students are in 4th grade.

---

6. Write a number sentence that uses $>$, $<$, or $=$ to compare the number of students in 4th grade with the number of students in 3rd grade.

________ ◯ ________

GO ON

Name ____________________

Yasmeen goes to Lincoln School. She counts the number of 2nd grade students who go there. The number in the circle is the total number of 2nd grade students at Lincoln School.

7. Fill in the missing numbers. Count by tens.

220, 230, ______, ______, ______, ______, ______

8. Yasmeen uses tens blocks to show the number of 2nd grade students. How many tens blocks will she need?

She will need ______ blocks.

9. Suppose Yasmeen's school has 210 students in 3rd grade. How would you figure out a number that is 10 more than that? Write your answer. Explain how you know.

____

____

____

____

GO ON

The number of students at Jefferson School is even. The number has three digits. The digit in the tens place is 4.

10. Write three numbers that could be the number of students at Jefferson School.

________ ________ ________

Explain how you know your answers are correct.

____

____

____

11. Choose one of the numbers that you just wrote. Write it three different ways.

12. Write a 3-digit number that could NOT be the number of students at Jefferson School.

There could NOT be ________ students.

STOP

1. Sally scores more points in a game than Ty.
Sally uses 900 − 500 to estimate how many more points.

Fill in the bubble next to all the problems she may have been estimating for.

○ $\begin{array}{r} 892 \\ -502 \\ \hline \end{array}$	○ $\begin{array}{r} 794 \\ -499 \\ \hline \end{array}$	○ $\begin{array}{r} 922 \\ -598 \\ \hline \end{array}$	○ $\begin{array}{r} 905 \\ -510 \\ \hline \end{array}$

2. Complete the equation that the diagram represents.

☐ + 17 = ☐

3. Use the data in the list to complete the line plot.

Lengths of Ribbons
7 inches
5 inches
7 inches
6 inches

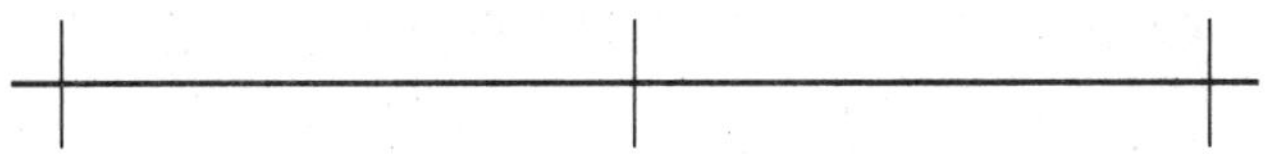

_______ _______ _______

____

4. Draw to show halves, thirds, and fourths.

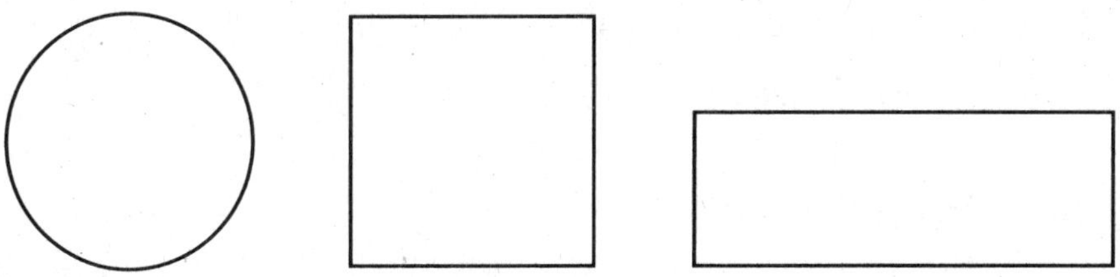

halves **thirds** **fourths**

GO ON

5. Draw and label coins to show a total value of 76¢.

6. Draw a picture to show how Jose can share 18 strawberries with his brother equally.

How many strawberries will Jose receive?

______ strawberries

7. Erin puts 3 small cans, 4 medium cans, and 5 large cans on a shelf. How many cans does she put on the shelf?

______ cans

8. Lara subtracts 73 from 188. Which one of these steps should she follow?

○ Ungroup 8 tens as 7 tens 10 ones.

○ Subtract 3 ones from 8 tens.

○ Subtract 7 tens from 8 tens.

GO ON

9. Use an inch ruler. What is the length of the paper clip to the nearest inch?

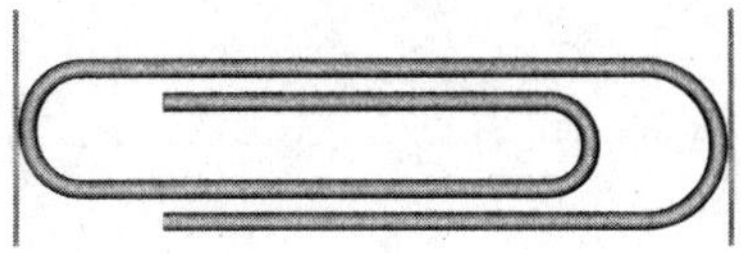

________ inches

---

10. Use the 1-inch mark. Estimate the length of each object.

about ______ inches

about ______ inches

---

11. Measure in centimeters. Draw rows and columns. Write the number of small squares.

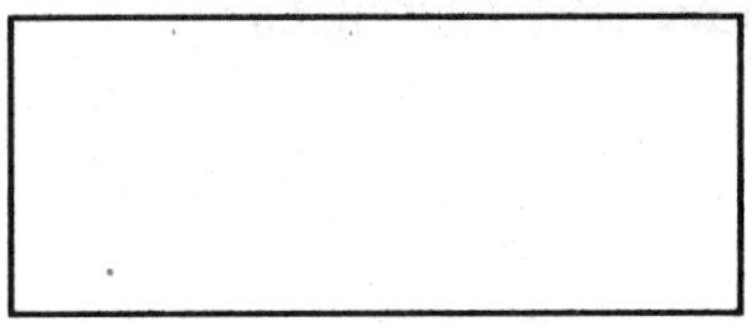

______ squares

GO ON

12. Megan counts by ones to 10. Lee counts by fives to 20. Who will say more numbers? Explain.

____

____

____

13. Mr. Polley puts a fence around his yard. The yard has three sides. One side is 12 feet long. The second side is 7 feet long. The third side is 15 feet long. How many feet of fence does he need?

______________ = ☐ ______________
unit

14. Use the words on the tiles to make the sentence true.

The table is 3 ________ long.

The belt is 30 ________ long.

The hallway is 15 ________ long.

inches feet

15. Shade in the ten frames to show the number. Circle **even** or **odd**.

18

even odd

GO ON

16. Ann has a favorite number. It has a digit less than 4 in the tens place. It has a digit greater than 6 in the ones place. Fill in the bubble next to all the numbers that could be Ann's number.

○ 30 + 9

○ sixty-seven

○ 2 tens 8 ones

Write another number that could be Ann's favorite.

______

---

17. Write a symbol from a tile to compare numbers.

$<$	$=$	$>$

152 ◯ 142

---

18. Find the difference.

$$\begin{array}{r} 90 \\ -\ 62 \\ \hline \end{array}$$

Tens	Ones
○ 2	○ 1
○ 3	○ 2
○ 5	○ 8

GO ON

19. Kevin drew 2 two-dimensional shapes that had 9 angles in all. Draw the shapes Kevin could have drawn.

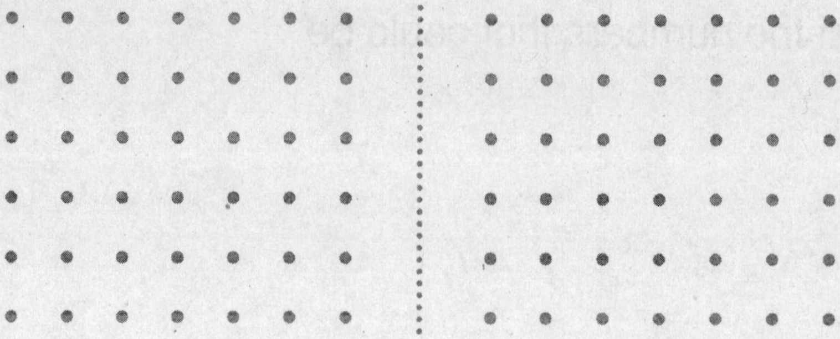

---

20. There are 4 boxes of 100 sheets of paper and some single sheets of paper in the closet. Choose all the numbers that show how many sheets of paper could be in the closet.

○ 348 ○ 324

○ 406 ○ 411

---

21. Ed has 28 blocks. Sue has 34 blocks. Who has more blocks? How many more? Label the bar model. Solve.

Circle the word and number from each box to make the sentence true.

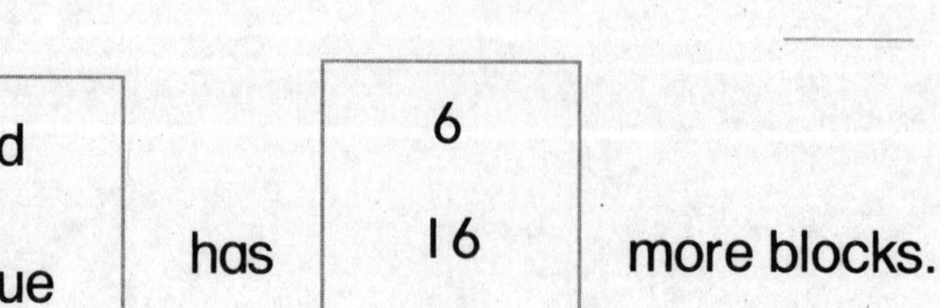

Ed Sue	has	6 16 52	more blocks.

GO ON

Name ____________________

22. Write the next number in each counting pattern.

214, 314, 414, 514, ______

123, 133, 143, 153, ______

---

23. Write the time that is shown on this clock.

____:____

---

24. Look at the bar graph. If Karina does 2 more sit-ups on Friday than she did on Thursday, how does the number of sit-ups change from Monday to Friday?

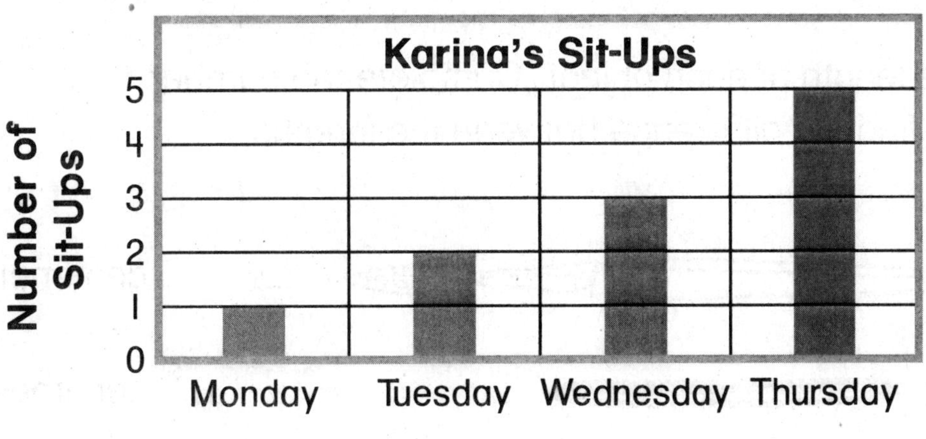

____

____

GO ON

Name ______________________________

25. Write how many tens. Circle groups of 10 tens.
Write how many hundreds. Write the number.

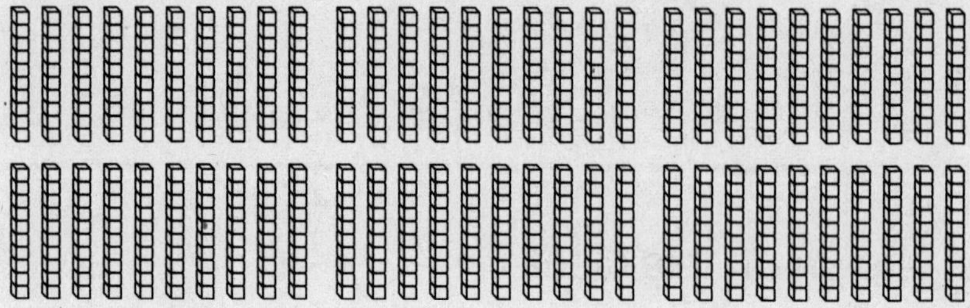

_____ tens

_____ hundreds

_____

26. Carlos has 23 red keys, 36 blue keys, and 44 green keys. How many keys does he have?

Carlos has [67 / 80 / 103] keys.

27. Measure the length of each object. Complete the number sentence to find the difference between the lengths.

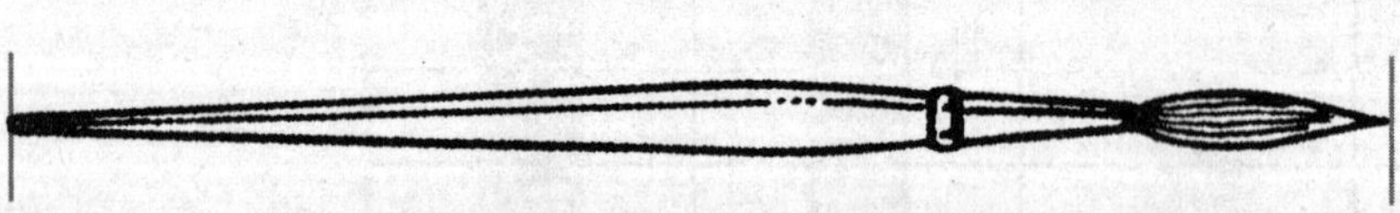

_____ centimeters

_____ centimeters

_____ − _____ = _____
centimeters centimeters centimeters

The paintbrush is _____ centimeters longer than the toothpick.

STOP

Name ______________________

The Reading Challenge

**Some children did a reading challenge.
They recorded how many books they read.**

1. Miguel read 7 books. Mia read the same number of books as Miguel. Write and solve the number sentence to show how many books Miguel and Mia read in all.

   _____ + _____ = _____

---

2. Abdul read 8 books. Jose read 11 books. How many more books did Jose read than Abdul?

   _____ books

---

3. Estela read 23 books last month. She put the books onto three shelves. Each shelf has a different number of books.

   Write a number sentence to show how many books might be on each shelf.

   _____ + _____ + _____ = _____

GO ON

Name ______________________

Middle-of-Year Performance Task

Franco read 22 books. Tia read 15 books. Ali read more books than Tia but fewer than Franco.

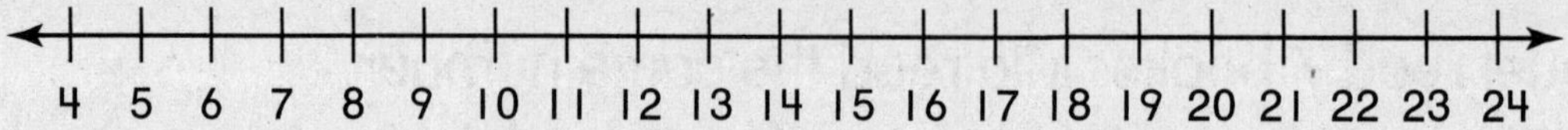

4. How many more books did Franco read than Tia? Use the number line to solve.

_______ books

5. How many books could the 3 children have read in all? Write a number sentence.

_______ + _______ + _______ = _______

Explain your answer.

____

____

____

GO ON

6. Erica read 31 books. Her friend Molly read 17 books. Draw a quick picture to show how many books Erica and Molly read in all.

They read ______ books in all.

---

7. Serena read a book that is 38 pages long. Ming read a book that is 26 pages long. Rohan read a book that is 31 pages long.

Ming finds how many pages he and Rohan read in all. How many more pages did they read than Serena?

They read ______ more pages than Serena.

Explain how you know your answer is correct.

____

____

____

____

____

GO ON

This tells how many books were read by all the children in 3 different classes.

Mr. Dorn's class	Ms. Lopez's class	Ms. Chen's class
319 books	185 books	241 books

8. How many books did the 3 classes read in all?

_______ books

9. How many more books did Mr. Dorn's class read than Ms. Lopez's class?

_______ books

10. The library has a shelf of storybooks. There are 473 new books on the shelf. The children at the school have already read 205 of these books. How many of the books have they NOT read yet?

_______ books

STOP

9. Use an inch ruler. What is the length of the marker to the nearest inch?

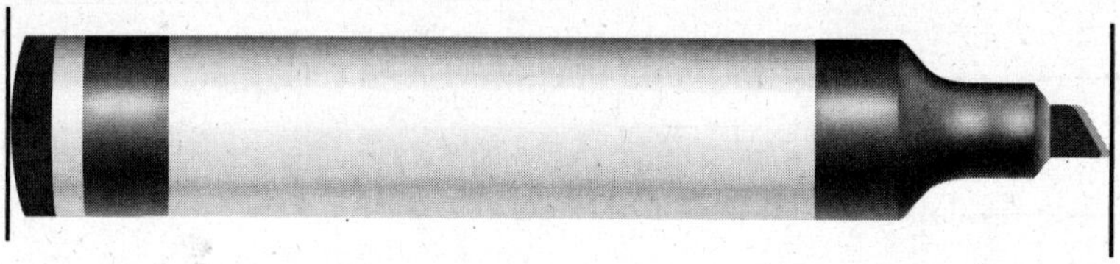

______ inches

10. Use the 1-inch mark. Estimate the length of each piece of yarn.

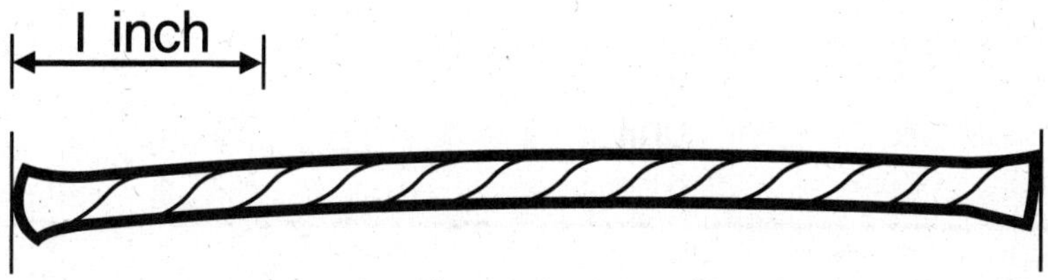

about ______ inches

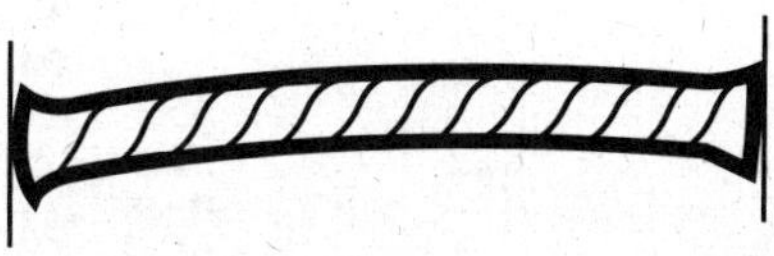

about ______ inches

11. Measure in centimeters. Draw rows and columns. Write the number of small squares.

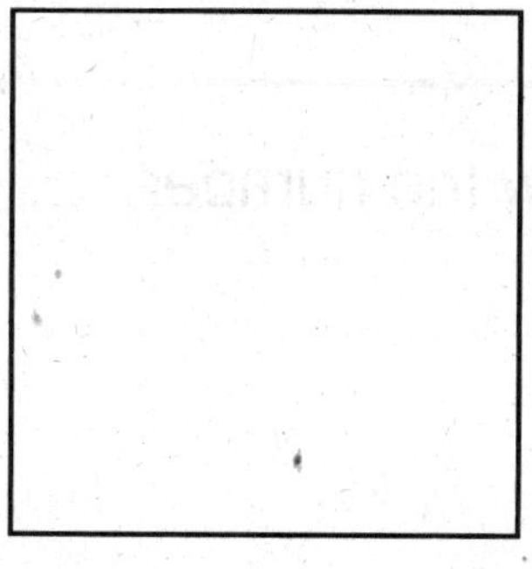

______ squares

GO ON

12. Arnod counts to 20 by fives. Bimi counts to 50 by tens. Who will say more numbers?

____

____

13. Sally puts a frame around a picture. The picture has four sides. Two sides are each 11 inches long. The other two sides are each 8 inches long. How many inches of frame does Sally need?

______________ = ☐ ________
unit

14. Use the words on the tiles to make the sentence true.

The tree is 18 ________ tall.

The desk is 30 ________ long.

The lamp is 3 ________ tall.

inches | feet

15. Shade in the ten frames to show the number. Circle **even** or **odd**.

20

even odd

GO ON

16. Jack's age has a digit less than 4 in the tens place. It has a digit greater than 6 in the ones place. Which one of these numbers could be Jack's age?

○ 40 + 9

○ thirty-seven

○ 2 tens 5 ones

Write a number that could be Jack's age.

______

---

17. Write a symbol from a tile to compare numbers.

<	=	>

136 ◯ 117

---

18. Find the difference.

$$\begin{array}{r} 61 \\ -\ 37 \\ \hline \end{array}$$

Tens	Ones
○ 2	○ 2
○ 3	○ 3
○ 4	○ 4

GO ON

19. Rana drew 2 two-dimensional shapes that had 10 angles in all. Draw the shapes Rana could have drawn.

---

20. A store has 3 boxes of 100 juice bottles and some single bottles. Circle all the numbers that show how many bottles could be in the store.

○ 348 ○ 324

○ 406 ○ 411

---

21. Ed has 44 stickers. Marcy has 53 stickers. Who has more stickers?

Circle the word or number from each box to make the sentence true.

Ed Marcy	has	19 11 9	more stickers.

GO ON

GO ON

22. Write the next number in each counting pattern.

885, 875, 865, 855, ______

641, 541, 441, 341, ______

23. Write the time that is shown on this clock.

______ : ______

24. Use the tally chart to complete the picture graph.
Draw a ☺ for each child.

Favorite School Subject	
math	||||
reading	|||
science	||
art	|||

Favorite School Subject					
math					
reading					
science					
art					

Key: Each ☺ stands for 1 child.

GO ON

25. Write how many tens. Circle groups of 10 tens. Write how many hundreds. Write the number.

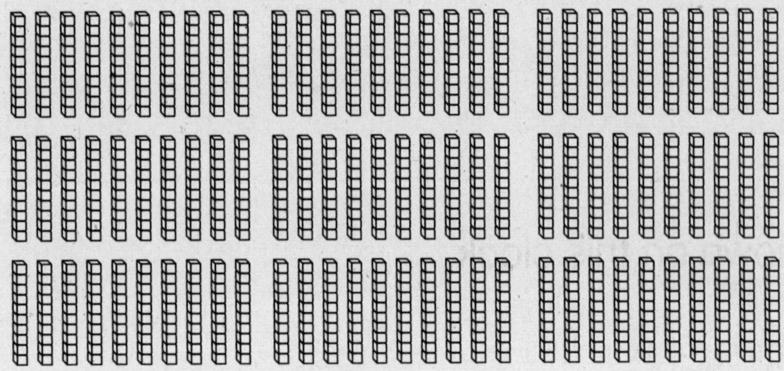

______ tens

______ hundreds

______

26. Hana picks 35 red apples, 16 green apples, and 27 yellow apples. How many apples does Hana pick?

Hana picks [65 / 78 / 84] apples.

27. Measure the length of each object. Complete the number sentence to find the difference between the lengths.

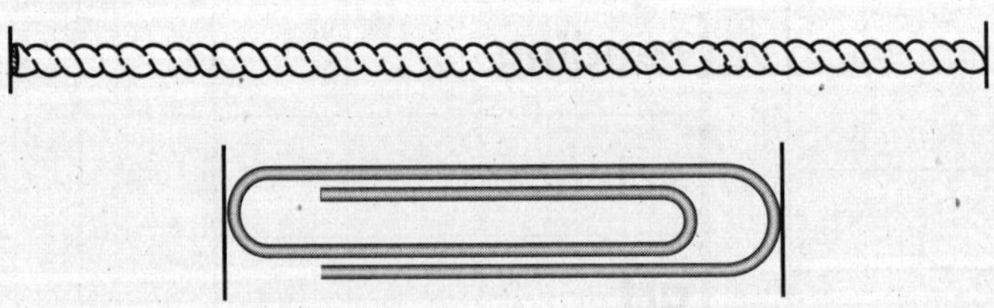

______ centimeters

______ centimeters

______ − ______ = ______

The string is ____ centimeters longer than the paper clip.

STOP

Name ______________________________

End-of-Year Performance Task

The Museum Store

1. The museum store opens at 10:00 A.M.
Eva gets to the store before 11:30 A.M.
Draw hands on the clock to show when
Eva might get to the store. Then write the time.

---

2. The clock shows when the store closes.
Write the time.

Is this an A.M. time or a P.M. time? Explain how you know.

____

____

____

GO ON

3. Jin buys a bookmark.
She uses these coins to pay for the bookmark.
How much does she pay?

_______ ¢

4. Jin also buys a pencil.
The pencil costs more than the bookmark.
The pencil costs less than one dollar.

How much could the pencil cost?

The pencil could cost _______ ¢.
Draw and label coins to show one way to make this amount.

5. Jin compares the lengths of her bookmark and her pencil. The pencil is about 12 cm long. What is a good estimate for the length of the bookmark?

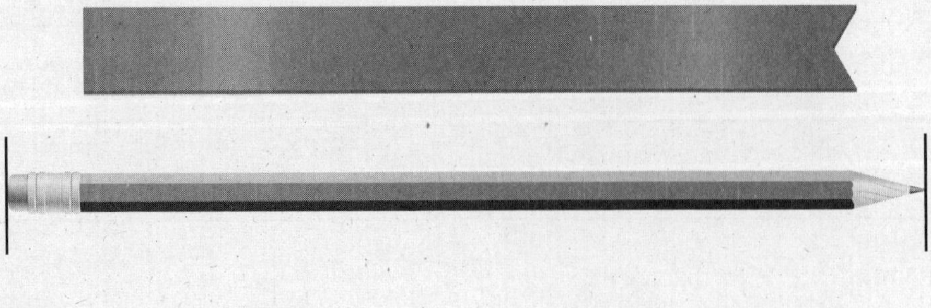

The bookmark is about _______ cm long.

GO ON

Name ______________________________

End-of-Year
Performance Task

The Museum Store

1. The museum store opens at 10:00 A.M.
Eva gets to the store before 11:30 A.M.
Draw hands on the clock to show when
Eva might get to the store. Then write the time.

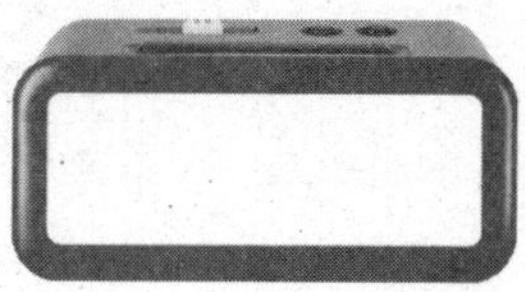

2. The clock shows when the store closes.
Write the time.

Is this an A.M. time or a P.M. time? Explain how you know.

____

____

____

GO ON

Name ______________________

3. Jin buys a bookmark.
She uses these coins to pay for the bookmark.
How much does she pay?

______ ¢

---

4. Jin also buys a pencil.
The pencil costs more than the bookmark.
The pencil costs less than one dollar.

How much could the pencil cost?

The pencil could cost ______ ¢.
Draw and label coins to show one way to make this amount.

---

5. Jin compares the lengths of her bookmark and her pencil. The pencil is about 12 cm long. What is a good estimate for the length of the bookmark?

The bookmark is about ______ cm long.

GO ON

The picture graph shows how many toy trucks of each color are in the store.

Colors of Trucks									
red	☺	☺	☺						
blue	☺	☺	☺	☺	☺				
black	☺	☺	☺	☺					
white	☺	☺	☺						

Key: Each ☺ stands for 1 truck.

---

6. How many black trucks are there? ______

---

7. Write color names to complete the sentence.

The number of ______ trucks is equal

to the number of ______ trucks.

---

8. The clerk sold 20 stuffed animals on Wednesday. He sold bears, lions, foxes, and turtles. Three of the animals were bears. Make a bar graph to show the stuffed animals.

Stuffed Animals Sold on Wednesday										
Animals										
Bear	(shaded)	(shaded)	(shaded)							
Lion										
Fox										
Turtle										
	0	1	2	3	4	5	6	7	8	9	10

Number of Animals Sold

GO ON

9. Grace buys a black pen at the store.

Use an inch ruler. Measure the length of the pen to the nearest inch.

The pen is about ______ inches long.

---

10. Grace also buys two banners for her room.
The first is 33 inches long. The second banner is 19 inches long.
How much longer is the first banner than the second banner?

______ – ______ = ______

______ inches longer

---

11. Grace uses this money to pay for her items.

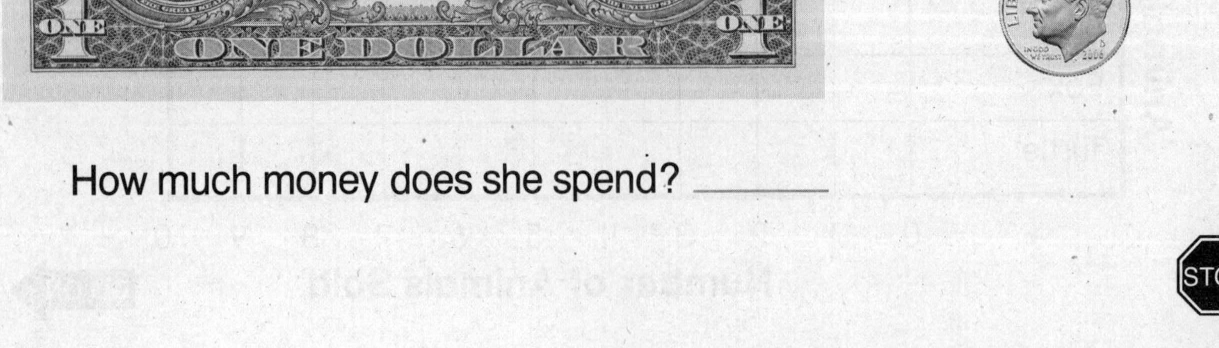

How much money does she spend? ______

STOP

Name ______________________

End-of-Year Performance Task

The picture graph shows how many toy trucks of each color are in the store.

Colors of Trucks									
red	☺	☺	☺						
blue	☺	☺	☺	☺	☺				
black	☺	☺	☺	☺					
white	☺	☺	☺						

Key: Each ☺ stands for 1 truck.

---

6. How many black trucks are there? ______

---

7. Write color names to complete the sentence.

The number of ______ trucks is equal

to the number of ______ trucks.

---

8. The clerk sold 20 stuffed animals on Wednesday. He sold bears, lions, foxes, and turtles. Three of the animals were bears. Make a bar graph to show the stuffed animals.

Animals	Stuffed Animals Sold on Wednesday									
Bear										
Lion										
Fox										
Turtle										
	0 1	2	3	4	5	6	7	8	9	10

Number of Animals Sold

GO ON

9. Grace buys a black pen at the store.

Use an inch ruler. Measure the length of the pen to the nearest inch.

The pen is about ______ inches long.

---

10. Grace also buys two banners for her room.
The first is 33 inches long. The second banner is 19 inches long.
How much longer is the first banner than the second banner?

______ – ______ = ______

______ inches longer

---

11. Grace uses this money to pay for her items.

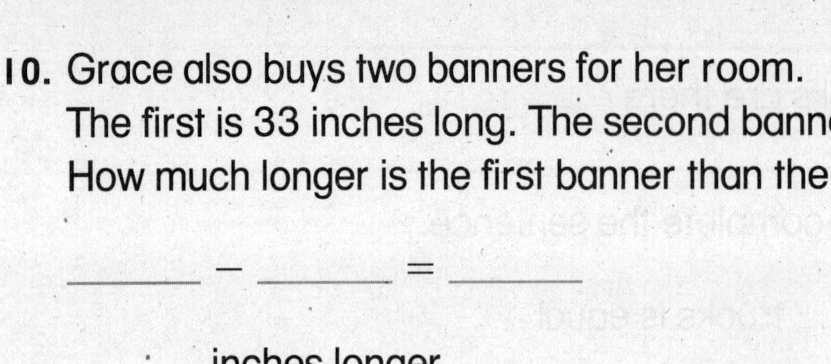

How much money does she spend? ______

STOP

Name ______________________________

End-of-Year Performance Task

The Museum Store

1. The museum store opens at 10:00 A.M.
Eva gets to the store before 11:30 A.M.
Draw hands on the clock to show when
Eva might get to the store. Then write the time.

2. The clock shows when the store closes.
Write the time.

Is this an A.M. time or a P.M. time? Explain how you know.

____

____

____

GO ON

3. Jin buys a bookmark.
She uses these coins to pay for the bookmark.
How much does she pay?

_______ ¢

4. Jin also buys a pencil.
The pencil costs more than the bookmark.
The pencil costs less than one dollar.

How much could the pencil cost?

The pencil could cost _______ ¢.
Draw and label coins to show one way to make this amount.

5. Jin compares the lengths of her bookmark and her pencil. The pencil is about 12 cm long. What is a good estimate for the length of the bookmark?

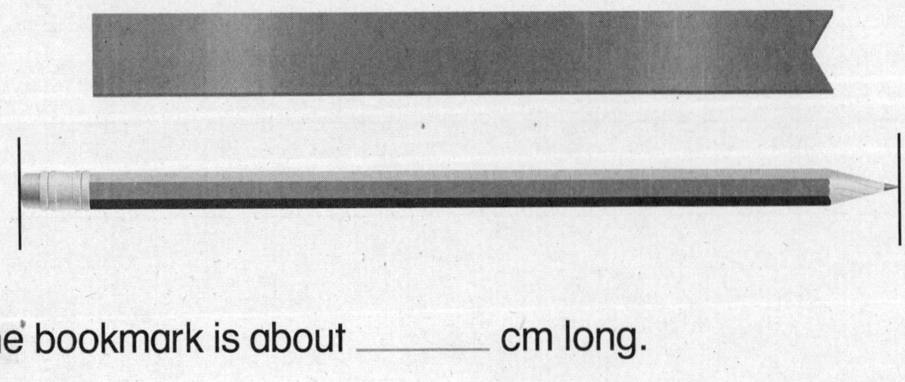

The bookmark is about _______ cm long.

GO ON

The picture graph shows how many toy trucks of each color are in the store.

Colors of Trucks									
red	☺	☺	☺						
blue	☺	☺	☺	☺	☺				
black	☺	☺	☺	☺					
white	☺	☺	☺						

Key: Each ☺ stands for 1 truck.

6. How many black trucks are there? ______

7. Write color names to complete the sentence.

The number of ______ trucks is equal

to the number of ______ trucks.

8. The clerk sold 20 stuffed animals on Wednesday. He sold bears, lions, foxes, and turtles. Three of the animals were bears. Make a bar graph to show the stuffed animals.

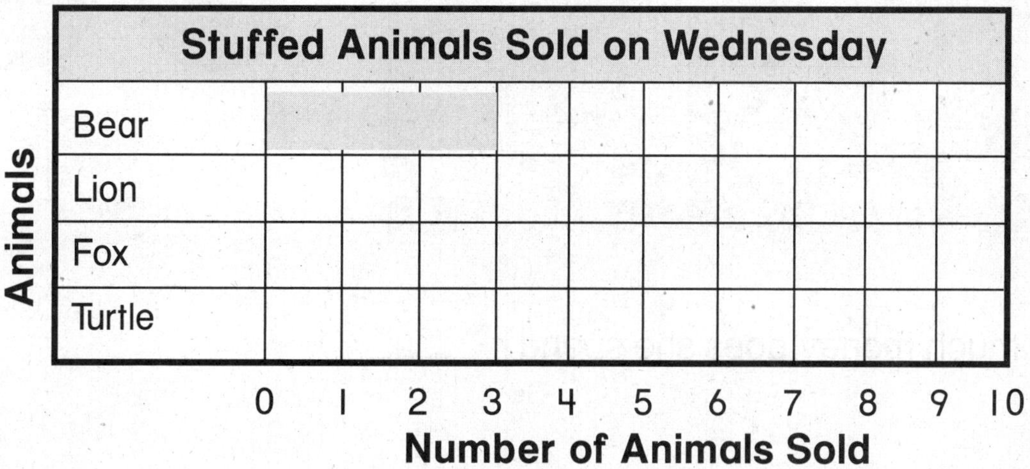

GO ON

Name ______________________________

End-of-Year Performance Task

9. Grace buys a black pen at the store.

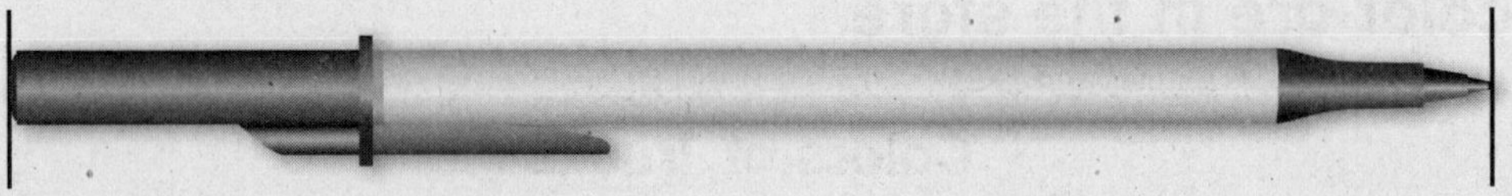

Use an inch ruler. Measure the length of the pen to the nearest inch.

The pen is about ______ inches long.

---

10. Grace also buys two banners for her room. The first is 33 inches long. The second banner is 19 inches long. How much longer is the first banner than the second banner?

______ − ______ = ______

______ inches longer

---

11. Grace uses this money to pay for her items.

How much money does she spend? ______

STOP